TWO WOMEN OF THE
GREAT SCHISM

The Other Voice in
Early Modern Europe:
The Toronto Series

SERIES EDITORS Margaret L. King *and* Albert Rabil, Jr.

Recent Publications in the Series

Two Women of the Great Schism:

The Revelations of Constance de Rabastens

by RAYMOND DE SABANAC

and

Life of the Blessed Ursulina of Parma

by SIMONE ZANACCHI

Edited and translated by

RENATE BLUMENFELD-KOSINSKI &
BRUCE L. VENARDE

ITER

Iter Inc.
Centre for Reformation and Renaissance Studies
Toronto
2010

Iter: Gateway to the Middle Ages and Renaissance
Tel: 416/978–7074   Fax: 416/971–1399

Email: iter@utoronto.ca   Web: www.itergateway.org

CRRS Publications, Centre for Reformation and Renaissance Studies
Victoria University in the University of Toronto
Toronto, Ontario M5S 1K7 Canada
Tel: 416/585–4465   Fax: 416/585–4430
Email: crrs.publications@utoronto.ca   Web: www.crrs.ca

We thank the Gladys Krieble Delmas Foundation for a generous grant of start-up funds for
The Other Voice in Early Modern Europe: The Toronto Series, a portion of which supports
the publication of this volume.

Library and Archives Canada Cataloguing in Publication
Two women of the Great Schism / edited and translated by Renate Blumenfeld-Kosinski &
Bruce L. Venarde.

(Other voice in early modern Europe : Toronto series ; 3)
Co-published by: Centre for Reformation and Renaissance Studies.
Includes bibliographical references and index.
Contents: The revelations of Constance de Rabastens / by Raymond de Sabanac — Life of
the Blessed Ursulina of Parma / by Simone Zanacchi.
Also available in electronic format.
ISBN 978-0-7727-2057-3
1. Constance, de Rabastens, fl. 1380–1386. 2. Ursulina, of Parma, Blessed, 1375–1410. 3.
Women in Christianity—History—Middle Ages, 600–1500. 4. Schism, The Great Western,
1378–1417. 5. Church history—Middle Ages, 600–1500. 6. Catholic Church—History. 7.
Visionaries—France—Biography. 8. Blessed—Italy—Biography. I. Blumenfeld-Kosinski,
Renate, 1952– II. Venarde, Bruce L., 1962- III. De Sabanac, Raymond. Revelations of
Constance de Rabastens IV.° Zanacchi, Simone. Life of the Blessed Ursulina of Parma
V.°Victoria University (Toronto, Ont.). Centre for Reformation and Renaissance Studies
VI. Iter Inc VII. Series: Other voice in early modern Europe. Toronto series ; 3

BX4705.C7735T86 2010
282.092'2   C2010–900621–6

Cover illustration: BEN 116355
Credit: The Legend of the True Cross, the Queen of Sheba Worshiping the Wood of the
Cross, detail of two female attendants, completed 1464 (fresco) by Francesca, Piero della, (c.
1415–92). San Francesco, Arezzo, Italy/ The Bridgeman Art Library. Nationality / copyright
status: Italian / out of copyright
Cover design: Maureen Morin, Information Technology Services, University of Toronto
Libraries
Typesetting and production: Iter Inc.

In honor of two foremothers

Elisabeth Blumenfeld (1916–2004)
and
Dell M. Trawick (1907–)

Contents

Acknowledgments

We have acquired many debts in the process of research and writing. For various kinds of help and information, we thank Jack Eckert, Alison Frazier, Marco Gentile, Silvia Guarnieri, Michael McCormick, Sharan Newman, Alessandra Talignani, Chad Taylor, and André Vauchez. Laura Smoller provided extremely insightful comments on an early draft of the Life of Ursulina of Parma that led to considerable reshaping of our introduction. Katherine McIver, an expert on San Quintino in Parma, sent evocative photos of Ursulina's tomb along with helpful bibliography. An anonymous reader minutely reviewed the entire manuscript, saving us from many small but embarrassing errors. Albert Rabil and Margaret King, co-editors of the Other Voice series, have borne with us through several stages of gestation. The editors would also like to gratefully acknowledge the support of the Richard D. And Mary Jane Edwards Endowed Publication Fund of the University of Pittsburgh.

The authors thank each other for the joy of scholarly—and other—companionship.

Renate Blumenfeld-Kosinski
Bruce L. Venarde

AASS: *Acta sanctorum quotquot toto orbe coluntur.* 68 volumes. Antwerp and Brussels: Société des Bollandistes, 1634–1940.

PL: *Patrologia cursus completus. Series latina.* Edited by J.-P. Migne. 221 volumes. Paris: J.-P. Migne, 1844–65.

Constance de Rabastens (active 1384–86) and Ursulina of Parma (1375–1408)

The Other Voice

It is not always possible to hear medieval women's voices directly. In many instances words and deeds were filtered through the writings of male authors. This was especially true for holy women who relied on their confessors to relay their visions and whose lives were written, sometimes posthumously, by male clerics. Such scenarios apply to the two women who take center stage in this volume, Constance de Rabastens (active 1384–86) and Ursulina of Parma (1375–1408). Although the texts we translate were written by men, they open an important window onto their protagonists' lives and works as well as the agency of women in the late Middle Ages. A large body of historical scholarship finds that European women's status, visibility, and opportunity eroded across the medieval centuries, leaving women victims of male oppression and even appropriation, to reprise the title of the series to which this book belongs, of their voices. It is difficult to arrive at coherent accounts of what Constance and Ursulina said and did, given that their actions are mediated through the genres of vision narrative and saint's life, written by Constance's confessor, Raymond de Sabanac, and by Ursulina's hagiographer, Simone Zanacchi, respectively. In that sense, learning about our two women of the Great Schism requires us to read against the grain, to try to peel away layers of editing and scripting to reveal an authentic core of female voice and experience.

However, some facts emerge that help us situate Constance and Ursulina in straightforward ways. Because of their forceful visionary and diplomatic interventions in the Great Schism, contemporaries took both women seriously enough to regard them as a threat to the political and ecclesiastical order, local and international. Constance and Ursulina managed to make their voices heard in a society that was dominated by men, and even in the extremely male-gendered spheres of secular politics and the Church hierarchy. Does that make them exceptional figures, or, as a male critic of the late-medieval author Christine de Pizan (c. 1364–c. 1430) described women who accomplished much in traditionally male-dominated spheres, freaks? We think not. Rather, the experiences of Constance and Ursulina show that whatever the rhetoric of female weakness and insignficance in late-medieval society—a rhetoric that can be deafening in the works of many male authors—the reality was rather different. Women could, especially if they were determined and intelligent, play important roles. Simply put, they made a difference to those around them, and for that reason alone, the challenges of sorting out the nature of their experiences, of pursuing hints and asides in the texts about them, are worth the trouble.

The presentation of a collection of revelations (with some letters) and a holy biography together may assist in what is necessarily an imaginative challenge. For Constance, we have vivid visions but little in the way of biographical detail; for Ursulina, we have a narrative account of her from birth to death that seems quite intentionally to shy away from detailed description of visionary experience. But read together, both with and against each other, our texts might offer a fuller view of women's experience. We can guess at the confusion and hostility with which the visionary Constance might have been received by reading about what everyone from neighbors to popes made of Ursulina, and we might heighten our understanding of Ursulina's rich interior religious life by reading about the (sometimes literally) colorful revelations of Constance. Did Constance ever travel? Did Ursulina ever see strange, brightly hued birds? These two women doubtless shared more than we can see from the historical record, given that they were similarly situated in time, social space, and religious perspectives. Had they ever met, they would have found a great deal to talk about. We moderns can worry too much about questions of mediation or manipulation by authors—for what written text is not at one remove from reality, from literal voice? What is certain is that the voices of these two women, and perhaps of many others of whom we have no documentary record, rang out loud and clear in their time. They mattered.

The texts presented in this book are very rich and thus demand some orientation. First, we briefly present the framework into which one can place our two protagonists: women's visionary experience and writings and the aspirations to holiness with a political twist. Then, we set the historical scene against which Constance of Rabastens and Ursulina of Parma played out their remarkable parts. There follows a concise biography of each woman along with consideration of the character of the writings from which our knowledge of their lives derives. Next comes some commentary on what may be the most surprising aspect of Constance's and Ursulina's activities: their very public and politically engaged actions. A final section considers the complex relationship of subjects and authors in these texts, the nature of which makes a true understanding of the women's stories and significance a real but—we hope—worthwhile challenge. History, spirituality, literary form, and gender are all important axes along which to ponder the experience of these two women of the Great Schism.

Constance and Ursulina's Foremothers

Throughout the Middle Ages, female visionaries could be found in many walks of life, in religious orders as well as among the laity. Many of these women lived lives of contemplation within the cloister walls or in the confines of *beguinages*, non-monastic communities of female spiritual seekers. Whatever the place, women established intimate relations with Christ or received privileged access to religious mysteries through their visions. Some of these women authored their own texts chronicling their visions and mystical experiences; others dictated them to scribes or confessors. Marie of Oignies (1177/78–1213), Mechthild of Magdeburg (d. 1282/87),[1] Beatrice of Nazareth (1200–1268), and Angela of Foligno (1248-1309) were women whose visionary experiences and writings centered on their interior lives.

But other women used their visions, at least in part, to try to intervene in the politico-religious conflicts of their time.[2] The earliest of these was the German Benedictine nun Hildegard of Bingen (1098–1179), who was not only aware of the political developments of her time but corresponded with rulers, such as the emperor Frederic Barbarossa, concerning the papal schism of 1159. Her younger contemporary Elisabeth of Schönau (1129–1165) also used some of her visionary experiences as a basis for various pronouncements on this schism.[3] Later on, we find female visionaries engaged in a variety

1. On the complex history of Mechthild's book and for a good introduction to women's religious writing see Sara S. Poor, *Mechthild of Magdeburg and Her Book: Gender and the Making of Textual Authority* (Philadelphia: University of Pennsylvania Press, 2004).

2. See André Vauchez, *The Laity in the Middle Ages: Religious Beliefs and Devotional Practice*, trans. Margery J. Schneider (Notre Dame: University of Notre Dame Press, 1993), chs. 18–19.

3. See Renate Blumenfeld-Kosinski, "Visions and Schism Politics in the Twelfth Century: Hildegard of Bingen, John of Salisbury, and Elisabeth of Schönau," in *Saints, Scholars, and*

of political missions. Margaret of Cortona (1247–97), for example, became famous in Tuscany as a preacher of peace and the crusade, while Clare of Montefalco (1268–1308) fought the heresy of the Free Spirit.[4]

The two women who can most be considered Constance and Ursulina's immediate foremothers are Birgitta of Sweden (1303–73) and Catherine of Siena (1347–80). They were among the very few female visionaries who were formally canonized, recognized as saints, although Catherine's canonization was not finalized until more than eighty years after her death. Birgitta, by contrast, was canonized no fewer than three times (in 1391, 1415, and 1417) by popes of different schismatic factions, the final time just at the end of the Great Schism. Her aristocratic background and the strong canonization lobby that sprung up around her undoubtedly account for the speediness of these proceedings.

Many female visionaries aroused suspicions of churchmen that made their canonizations, if not impossible, problematic. In fact, the famous French theologian Jean Gerson (1363–1429) challenged Birgitta's canonization at the Council of Constance in 1415 and seemed to target Birgitta and Catherine when in 1423, six years after the end of the Great Schism, he looked back on the 1377 decision of Pope Gregory XI to return to Rome (which may have contributed to the Schism: see below) and blamed the undue influence visionaries had on this pope.[5] It is within this contentious climate regarding visionary activity and aspirations to holiness that we have to place our portagonists.

How did Birgitta and Catherine attempt to intervene in the politics of their time? We can give only the briefest summary of their complex roles here. Birgitta, a Swedish widow of aristocratic origin and a mother of eight, used her visionary authority to speak out concerning the Hundred Years' War between England and France and sent messages to the Swedish king as well as Pope Clement VI when war resumed in 1346. She then moved to Rome and toward the end

Politicians: Gender as a Tool in Medieval Studies, ed. Mathilde van Dijk and Renée Nip (Turnhout: Brepols, 2005), 173–87.

4. See Peter Dinzelbacher, *Mittelalterliche Frauenmystik* (Paderborn: F. Schöningh, 1993), ch. 10.

5. Although Gerson actually says "male as well as female visionaries." See Renate Blumenfeld-Kosinski, *Poets, Saints, and Visionaries of the Great Schism, 1378–1417* (University Park: State University of Pennsylvania Press, 2006) 34 and n. 10. Dyan Elliott sees Gerson's words as part of a "major campaign against female mysticism." See *Proving Woman: Female Spirituality and Inquisitional Culture in the Later Middle Ages* (Princeton: Princeton University Press, 2004), 264; see 268 for Gerson's challenge at Constance.

of her life was especially vocal in her campaign to persuade popes Urban V (1362–70) and Gregory XI (1370–78) to return the papal see from Avignon to Rome.[6] On one occasion, after a vision Birgitta told Gregory XI that the devil retained him in Avignon and that his love for Christ had grown cold, that he was a paralytic corrupted by cold blood and humor, and that this paralysis prevented him from moving to Rome.[7] Despite these exhortations, the pope did not consent to leaving Avignon and Birgitta died before the ardently desired return to Rome became reality.

Catherine of Siena, twenty-third child of a Sienese dyer and thus a member of the artisan class, played a political role that was more important than that of any other holy woman of her time. In 1374 she met the future master general of the Dominican Order, Raymond of Capua, who became her spiritual advisor and biographer. Like Birgitta, Catherine agitated for the papacy's return to Rome; in fact, she functioned as a successor to Birgitta and her advisory mission after Pope Gregory XI contacted her through Birgitta's confessor, Alfonso of Pecha. Before the beginning of the Great Schism, Catherine's major political involvement concerned the conflict between the republic of Florence and the papacy as well as the numerous other hostilities between the different Italian city-states.[8]

Catherine's rhetoric urging Gregory XI to move to Rome was forceful and picturesque. In one letter dating from 1376, for example, she told Gregory that his egoism kills virtue—which then resembles the stillborn baby of an unfortunate mother. Somewhat later, she writes "Up, Father! No more irresponsibility!"[9] Gregory returned to Rome in 1377. It is hard to judge how important a role Catherine played in his decision, which was motivated by a whole host of political and ecclesiastical considerations. Jean Gerson, as we just saw, seemed to blame Catherine and Birgitta for Gregory's return to the eternal city. A fifteenth-century painting by Benvenuto di Giovanni

---

6. For her biography and political roles see Claire L. Sahlin, *Birgitta of Sweden and the Voice of Prophecy* (Rochester, NY: Boydell Press, 2001) and on the return to Rome, Blumenfeld-Kosinski, *Poets, Saints, and Visionaries*, 36–42.

7. See Blumenfeld-Kosinski, *Poets, Saints, and Visionaries*, 40. Birgitta here refers to the medical theory of the humors, which were believed to govern people's temperaments.

8. F. Thomas Luongo, *The Saintly Politics of Catherine of Siena* (Ithaca: Cornell University Press, 2006).

9. *The Letters of Catherine of Siena*, ed. Suzanne Noffke, 2 vols. (Tempe: Arizona Center for Medieval and Renaissance Studies, 2000), 1:246 and 249.

in the Ospedale di S. Maria della Scala in Siena shows Catherine leading Pope Gregory XI in a splendid procession entering the city of Rome, confirming the belief of a sizable group of people that the saint had indeed been instrumental in this momentous return.[10] After the pope's return to Rome and the beginning of the Great Schism in 1378, Catherine's became one of the loudest voices urging the reunification of the Church. Her passionate letters to European rulers, cardinals, and the Roman pope Urban VI are extraordinary examples of saintly eloquence put to political use.[11] Sadly, none of her reasonable proposals were heeded, none of her impassioned pleas acted on: the Great Schism was to divide the Church for another generation.

Raymond of Capua wrote Catherine's first life, the *Legenda maior*, between 1385 and 1395; Thomas Caffarini penned a second account, the *Legenda minor*, in the early fifteenth century; and between 1411 and 1416 the *Processo castellano*, part of the Dominican campaign in support of Catherine's canonization, gathered numerous testimonies to her holiness. Unlike Birgitta's case, confirmed three times in twenty-six years, Catherine's dossier languished, and it was not until 1461 that the Sienese pope Pius II canonized his hometown's saint.[12] It is possible that the nuns of San Quintino were inspired by this event to begin thinking about the canonization of the holy woman buried in their church, their very own Ursulina of Parma.

How can we explain the emergence into the public arena of our two eloquent women? Daniel Bornstein suggests that eras that see "cracks in ecclesiastical structures" are especially open to "female influence and to experimentation with novel religious roles." He states:

> It was during the long decades of the Avignon papacy and of the Great Schism, when the validity of any particular religious authority was rendered doubtful, first by the removal of the papacy from its proper seat [i.e., from Rome to Avignon] and then by the spectacle of two (and later three) competing hierarchies, that women like St. Catherine of Siena, St. Birgitta of Sweden,

---

10. The painting is reproduced in the *Bibliotheca sanctorum* 3:1002 (Rome: Pontificia Università lateranense, 1963).

11. For an analysis of her letters relating to the papacy's return to Rome and her attempts to end the Schism see Blumenfeld-Kosinski, *Poets, Saints, and Visionaries*, 42–54.

12. In 1939 Catherine was named one of the patrons of Italy and in 1970 she was declared a doctor of the Church.

and lesser figures were able to emerge as vociferous protagonists of the religious life. It was when the male hierarchy was in obvious disarray that prominent churchmen were most willing to listen to strange voices, disregard decorum and timeworn proprieties, and concede these women a place at (or near) the altar.[13]

Constance de Rabastens and Ursulina of Parma thus fit into a lineage of politically engaged visionaries, women who used their supernatural experiences and their charisma to create voices that allowed them to speak to the rulers and prelates of their time, either judging them and consigning some of them to hell (as did Constance) or actively pursuing diplomatic efforts through untiring travel between Rome and Avignon (as did Ursulina). The Great Schism laid bare the fissures in ecclesiastical authority Bornstein describes. But it was not only female visionaries who felt authorized and compelled to speak out against the pope they considered illegitimate. The same period also saw some male visionaries engaged in seeking support, through their revelations, for one or the other pope. The prime example of a male visionary in this role, Friar Pedro of Aragon (1305–81), was a highly placed Franciscan and the uncle of the king of Aragon. That his counsel to support the Roman pope was not heeded by his nephew was not due to his gender but to the political expediency that finally moved all the Spanish kingdoms to adhere to the Avignon pope.

Still, it is safe to say that our two women, of different backgrounds but motivated by similar missions, were aided by the spiritual uncertainty and crisis of authority of their era when they wanted to make their voices heard. The same goes for Marie Robine (d. 1399), a peasant woman from the Pyrenees who settled in Avignon and became spokeswoman for the Avignon popes Clement VII and Benedict XIII. The latter even sent her to Paris in 1398 to persuade the French king not to withdraw obedience from his papacy. The

13. Daniel Bornstein, "Women and Religion in Late Medieval Italy: History and Historiography," in Daniel Bornstein and Roberto Rusconi, ed., *Women and Religion in Medieval and Renaissance Italy* (Chicago: University of Chicago Press, 1996), 6. For a slightly later period, the early sixteenth century, Gabriella Zarri traces the fates of fourteen women who in many ways can be seen as descendants of our two women: their revelations and prophecies were adapted to the political problems of their own time and they frequently found the ear of the rulers of the many different Italian states. See Gabriella Zarri, "Living Saints: A Typology of Female Sanctity in the Early Sixteenth Century," in Bornstein and Rusconi, ed., *Women and Religion in Medieval and Renaissance Italy*, 219–303.

crisis occasioned by disputes between this pope and the king thus enabled Marie to become a papal ambassador. Her mission, however, ended in failure and led to her disillusionment with the papacy she had so fervently served and revered earlier.[14] It is likely that women of the background and social class of these three women—whether a small-town widow like Constance, a peasant woman like Marie, or a member of the urban middle class as was Ursulina—would not have had the ear of churchmen had the Great Schism not caused political upheavals and doubts about the continued authority of the Church in the regions they inhabited.

In order to demonstrate in more detail the seriousness of the issues with which they chose to engage, we will take a closer look at the Great Schism, the grave crisis that divided the Church into two and eventually three factions for thirty-nine years.

The Great Schism: Christendom Divided

For over a generation the Great Schism (1378–1417), pitting first two and then three popes against each other, divided Christian Europe. During most of the fourteenth century the papacy had resided in Avignon, and all the popes from Clement V (1304–14) to Gregory XI (1370–78) were of French or Occitan origin. In the second half of the century more and more voices—poetic, prophetic, and diplomat-ic—clamored for a return of the papacy to Rome. Birgitta of Sweden (1303–73), Catherine of Siena (1347–80), and Friar Pedro of Aragon as well as the poet Petrarch (1304–74) were among those urging the pope to move his see back to Rome. Finally, in 1377, Pope Gregory XI decided to undertake the fateful move to Rome. But already in March 1378 Gregory was dead, and the papal election that occurred a month later caused one of the most profound crises the Western Church had ever experienced.[15] The conclave of the sixteen cardinals trying to choose a new pope was surrounded by a mob of armed Romans who demanded an Italian pope. The cardinals, after much deliberation,

---

14. On Marie Robine see Matthew Tobin, "Les Visions et révélations de Marie Robine d'Avignon dans le contexte prophétique des années 1400," in *Fin du monde et signes des temps. Visionnaires et prophètes en France méridionale (fin XIIIe–début XVe siècle). Cahiers de Fanjeaux* 27 (1992), 309–29 and Blumenfeld-Kosinski, *Poets, Saints, and Visionaries*, esp. 81–85.

15. See Walter Ullmann, *The Origins of the Great Schism* (London: Burns, Oates & Wash-bourne, 1948).

agreed on the archbishop of Bari, Bartolomeo Prignano, who took office as Pope Urban VI.

Urban soon showed his true nature, as the cardinals later complained. Autocratic and irascible, he began to curtail the cardinals' autonomy and the luxurious lifestyle they had imported from Avignon. In response, the cardinals left Rome in the summer of 1378 and took refuge in Anagni. Here, in the month of September, they proceeded to elect another pope, claiming that the April election was invalid because there had been no liberty of choice in face of the menacing throngs outside the conclave. Their new choice was Robert of Geneva, a relative of the French king Charles V, who quickly accepted the papal tiara as Pope Clement VII, and, after various troubles, settled in the impressive papal fortress in Avignon. Thus, within the space of five months the same group of cardinals had elected two different popes.

This unprecedented event had immediate political repercussions, since every European ruler had to choose one or the other pope. England adhered from the beginning to Pope Urban VI, while the French monarchy—after some deliberation—not surprisingly chose the Frenchman Clement VII. Spain, after protracted inquiries into the true circumstances of the double election, eventually opted for Clement VII, as did Scotland, while the Empire and the Italian region preferred the Roman pope. Flanders remained divided.

At the moment Constance de Rabastens (active 1384–86) and Ursulina of Parma (1375–1408) appeared on the scene, the Schism had become entrenched and no solution seemed to be at hand. There is no doubt that the division of the Church caused great anxiety to Christians from all walks of life. Contemporary chroniclers, such as Michel Pintoin, the chronicler of Saint-Denis in Paris, give many examples of the doubts and anguish that ordinary Christians experienced in the face of two popes whose open hostility toward each other included military action and mutual anathema.[16] Our two women were among those Christians who, by divine command, attempted to intervene in the crisis of the Church.

---

16. See Blumenfeld-Kosinski, *Poets, Saints, and Visionaries* for many examples of this anxiety and for the responses offered by writers and artists in different countries and milieus. The chronicler of Saint-Denis had his finger on the pulse of the French people; indeed Bernard Guenée uses this chronicle as the touchstone for public opinion at the time in his fascinating study *L'opinion publique à la fin du Moyen Age d'après la "Chronique de Charles VI" du Religieux de Saint-Denis* (Paris: Perrin, 2002).

Constance hailed from Languedoc, a region that had seen some turmoil just prior to the onset of Constance's visionary activity. Languedoc had become a French crown territory in the early thirteenth century, following on the cruel and destructive Albigensian crusade, which, though proclaimed to be a campaign against heretics, was in fact a move to enlarge the domain of the French king. After the death of King Charles V in 1380, Languedoc was supposed to come under the administration of the Count of Foix-Béarn, Gaston Fébus (1331–91). But the regents, Charles V's brothers, who took over for Charles's twelve-year-old son, contravened the late king's orders and appointed one of their own allies to the position. Defeated in armed resistance, Gaston Fébus renounced the lieutenancy of Languedoc but held on to his own territories of Foix-Béarn.

Being under the domination of the French crown, Languedoc embraced the Avignon pope Clement VII. But the attitude of the count of Foix resembled the wait-and-see stance of the Spanish kingdoms and then evolved into one of neutrality, although he did require a tithe in favor of the Avignon pope.[17] Constance admired the count of Foix, yet her visions endorse the Roman pope, a contradiction that for her clearly needed no resolution.

But Europe was divided not only by the Great Schism. For two decades, France and England had been pitted against each other in the Hundred Years' War. Constance was as aware of this conflict as she was of the Schism. Several times (in Chapter 2.23 and Letter 6) she speaks of Flanders, a contested region, although she seems to have misunderstood the political situation. The cities of Flanders had risen up against their count, Louis de Male, and had shown pro-English leanings. In response, the new French king, fourteen-year-old Charles VI, invaded Flanders, in a military campaign styled as a "crusade" aimed at eradicating revolt and heresy (that is, adherence to the Roman pope) and at forestalling any alliance with the English enemy. Constance rightly sees Flanders as the French king's enemy, yet Flanders for the most part supports the Roman pope, the one favored by Constance. Therefore, Constance's statement in Letter 6 ("Flanders … will be punished for the persecution") contradicts some of her other statements of support for one or the other side. Thus she admires and seems concerned about the young king of France even though he adheres to the Avignon pope whom Constance considers

17. See Pierre Tucoo-Chala, *Gaston Fébus et la vicomté de Béarn, 1343-1391* (Bordeaux: Bière, 1959), 328–29.

the devil incarnate. Clearly, Constance's papal and monarchical allegiances are at irreconcilable odds.

We must read the political portions of Constance's *Revelations* against this multifaceted background at the end of a troubled century. On the one hand, Constance supported the young French king Charles VI despite his support of the "wrong" pope. On the other, she idolized the Count of Foix, whose leanings were also pro-Clement and even somewhat pro-English. As for the situation in Flanders, Constance was aware of some crisis there, but she never articulated any coherent opinion on the Flemish problems. Constance's views of the events of her time were not always accurate or even consistent, but they do betray a passionate desire to intervene in the politics of the day on the part of an ordinary woman from the south of France.

In Italy, too, the Schism cast a long shadow over political affairs. Not a united nation-state until the nineteenth century, the Italian peninsula was from ancient times a land of cities. One of these was Parma, lying at the crossing of two streams in the enormous flood plain of the Po River in northern Italy.[18] The city was on the Via Emilia, the major Roman thoroughfare that ran along the southern edge of the Po Valley. Parma declined in the late Roman era, but attained new economic and strategic importance in the early Middle Ages, eventually coming under the dominion of emperors from north of the Alps. In the clashes between emperors and popes in the central Middle Ages, however, Parma ended up siding with Rome and soon after, like many Italian cities, established a communal form of government that, despite the ideal of a commune as an alliance of various citizen interests, remained largely under the control of a small group of wealthy families for centuries. Intense competition between several prominent families in the fourteenth century, economic and fiscal troubles, and even famine led finally to the takeover Parma by the powerful Visconti lords of Milan, a city 75 miles to the northwest, in 1346. When Ursulina was born in 1375, the city was under the rule of Galeazzo II Visconti, succeeded shortly afterwards by his son Gian Galeazzo, who increased the already large territory centered in Milan by extending control over cities to the east and south, into the Apennine mountain region of central Italy.

In the period around Ursulina's lifetime there emerged the general pattern of late-medieval and Renaissance Italian political

---

18. A standard account is Ferdinando Bernini, *Storia di Parma*, 2nd edition (Parma: L. Battei, 1976).

organization: five major city-states (Milan, Venice, Florence, the papal states centered in Rome, and Naples) that controlled most other cities in a dizzying succession of alliances, conflicts, and realignments. When the Great Schism began, Ursulina was three years old. The northern city-states, Milan, Venice, and Florence, remained loyal to the Roman papacy, of which they were the political rivals. The situation in Naples was different, however, since the rulers of that city and its large territory in southern Italy had strong ties to France, whose royal family had pan-European connections by blood and marriage.[19] Joanna I, queen of Naples 1343–82, was descended on both sides from French royalty; her colorful life included four marriages, numerous challenges to her legitimacy from relatives in Italy and Hungary, and several periods of sole rule. When Urban VI, formerly the archbishop of Bari and thus Joanna's subject, was elected pope in 1378, he promptly announced plans to support a Hungarian claim to the throne of Naples. When Clement VII was elected as a rival to Urban VI, Joanna took the Avignon side in the schism. Joanna died as a prisoner in 1382 during the ensuing civil war, waiting to be rescued by her designated heir, Louis of Anjou, uncle and former regent of the French king Charles VI so revered by Constance of Rabastens. Queen Joanna's successor (an adopted son and perhaps also her assassin, since her death was probably murder) was another Charles, crowned king by none other than the Roman pope Urban VI, who had supported his claim to the throne. Charles died only a few years later and was succeeded by his son Ladislas. Ladislas, an adherent of the Roman papacy, spent his reign of almost thirty years—covering the rest of Ursulina's lifetime— locked in struggle with another rival claimant, this one the son of Joanna's final choice as heir, Louis of Anjou.

In short, while most of Italy remained loyal to the Roman papacy, it was also centered geographically between the Avignon-loyal French kingdom and Naples, where political rivalries and dynastic struggles were always linked to support for rival popes. In Italian politics at the time, nothing was entirely predictable, in regions or individual cities. Although it was not until much later that a French king actually led an army into Italy, the constant presence of members of the French royal house on the peninsula throughout the period of the schism meant that the Avignon popes had powerful allies to the south of Rome.

19. See Tommaso Astarita, *Between Salt Water and Holy Water: A History of Southern Italy* (New York: Norton, 2005), 54–85, for a sketch of southern Italy in the later Middle Ages.

At least as important as the geopolitical landscape, though, was Ursulina's immediate environment in her native city. Despite remains of a Roman theater and amphitheater, she probably attached more importance to the religious structures in Parma, for example, the Romanesque cathedral consecrated in the early twelfth century and a distinctive octagonal baptistery built a century later. But there were many other churches in Parma, parishes serving city neighborhoods and the churches of various religious groups of monks, canons, friars, and nuns. One of the latter was San Quintino, the monastery church of a community of nuns established in the twelfth century. It was at San Quintino that Ursulina's body was buried after her death; and it was there, around those holy relics, that a cult developed in the course of the fifteenth century, encouraged by the account of her life Simone Zanacchi wrote in 1472 at the behest of Abbess Magdalena Sanvitale.

Constance de Rabastens and her Revelations

Little is known for certain about Constance de Rabastens.[20] All our information comes from her revelations as they were transcribed by her confessor, Raymond de Sabanac. Her earliest vision deals with the death of her husband; in Chapter 2.15 Constance mentions a daughter; and in 2.20 we learn that her son was a Benedictine monk in Toulouse and wrote some texts for her. A heading in the unique manuscript informs us that Constance was at one point in prison. While the exterior circumstances of her life remain mostly unknown we learn much about her rich interior life through her revelations.

The transcription of her revelations made by Raymond de Sabanac, possibly a law professor from Toulouse, was probably originally in Latin or Provençal. Today it exists only in medieval Catalan in manuscript Bibliothèque nationale de France, latin 5055 (folios 35 recto to 58 recto). The editors, Valois and Pagès, believe that the writing comes from late fourteenth-century Rousillon, an area that was then part of Aragon.[21] Constance's revelations and letters appear in no strict chronological order. We first read a preface that lays out the principles of the discernment of spirits, a set of rules

20. The lively scenes of Constance's village life and her interactions with others described in Jean-Pierre Hiver-Bérenguier's *Constance de Rabastens: Mystique de Dieu ou de Gaston Febus?* (Toulouse: Privat, 1984) are pure fantasy.

21. See Noël Valois and Amédée Pagès, "Les Révélations de Constance de Rabastens et le Schisme d'Occident (1384–86)," *Annales du Midi* 8 (1896), 242.

that was devised in the later Middle Ages to "test" visions for their authenticity.[22] Here Raymond assures us that Constance's revelations met all the appropriate criteria. Then follows a long series of visions as told to Raymond, complemented by some visions told to her son and then transmitted to Raymond; finally we find six letters from Constance to the inquisitor in Toulouse, probably written for her by her son. All the other texts in the manuscript are in Latin and deal with a variety of subjects, including treatises by historians and by some of the Church Fathers as well as a text on anatomy and a treatise on games. Since a number of the folios are bound upside down in this codex, one wonders about how and by what rationale it was put together. In any case, the folios containing Constance's revelations stand out by their beautiful writing and rather clean pages in an otherwise quite dirty and even torn codex.

How can one define the genre of Constance's text? It is not a purely mystical text in the sense that meditations on Christ's suffering and the desire of joining herself to Christ are not at the center of her text, though they are undeniably present. Nor is there any easily defined doctrinal content. Central to the *Revelations* is rather Constance's political mission: to denounce the Avignon pope as a usurper and to persuade the clerical and secular authorities of the region around Toulouse to adhere to the Roman pope. A divine power sends her dramatic revelations and a divine voice instructs her how to interpret the striking scenes that appear before her eyes and at the same time provides her with a script for her communications with the bishop of Toulouse and his entourage. Biblical echoes (especially from the Book of Revelation) and imagery inspired by these texts give a scriptural authority to the messages Constance is ordered to disseminate to those around her.[23] Thus by far the most common command Constance receives is "Write this down and transmit it to…" (e.g., 2.22, 2.33 2.37, 2.48, 2.62). The voice does not always name the person to whom Constance's writings should be addressed. Sometimes it is a general order indicating that writing down her revelations will profit the people; at other times the voice names the intended recipient, for example, the inquisitor in Toulouse.

22. See Nancy Caciola, *Discerning Spirits: Divine and Demonic Possession in the Middle Ages* (Ithaca: Cornell University Press, 2003) and Elliott, *Proving Woman.*

23. These biblical intertexts become much more numerous after section 2.30, perhaps because Constance's revelations became more and more threatening to the ecclesiastical authorities and therefore needed increased legitimization.

The divine voice insists again and again on Constance's election to this mission and on the fact that she is a woman. Her gender allows for identification with a number of female biblical figures, such as the Virgin Mary, whose disconsolate state Constance is said to imitate (2.44 and 57; see John 19:25) or the woman "clothed in the sun" in Revelation 12, who is given wings and transported into the desert in order to escape from the threatening serpent (2.41; see Rev. 12:14). But most striking is the voice's recognition that as an unlearned woman, Constance has never studied the Scriptures (2.32, 2.63, and Letter 4). Nonetheless she is called upon by Christ to explain the Scriptures to learned men, a task that is as sacred as it is risky (2.63).

As her revelations multiply and her confessor transcribes and circulates them, Constance's reputation as a visionary spreads. For some she becomes a kind of oracle to be consulted on political questions, such as the significance of the duke of Anjou's death (2.45), or how much longer the Great Schism might last (2.46) and whether the end of the world is near (2.47). But for the clerical authorities she becomes a major nuisance, a simple woman who attempts to play a public role denouncing the Church's policies. Her visions of the Avignon pope and his cardinals burning in hell prove to be intolerable to the authorities in Toulouse and Constance ends up in jail, as we learn at the beginning of Part 3. But imprisonment does not silence our outspoken visionary—she now uses her son to carry her messages to the inquisitor of Toulouse, Hugues de Verdun. What ultimately happened to Constance is not known. Her revelations were preserved, in but a single manuscript and only in a Catalan translation. It is possible that this translation was made so that it could circulate in Aragon as part of the pro-Urban VI propaganda, a movement that tried to persuade the Spanish kingdoms, which had not yet decided who was the rightful pope, to rally themselves to the Roman pope.[24]

Ursulina of Parma and her Vita

We have far more detailed knowledge of the life Ursulina of Parma, most of it from the Latin biography written over sixty years after her

---

24. See Blumenfeld-Kosinski, *Poets, Saints, and Visionaries of the Great Schism*, 63. Another saintly personage, Pedro of Aragon (1305–81), a Franciscan friar and uncle of the Aragonese king, was also engaged in pro-Urban VI propaganda (ibid., 55–59).

death. The author of this *vita*, or saint's life, was Simone Zanacchi.[25] In the first section of the *vita* he lists the Latin and vernacular sources he drew on for his work. Zanacchi was a member of the austere Carthusian order of monks and nuns who combined communal and hermit-like existences in their communities. He had entered monastic life in Parma and risen to be prior, that is, head of a Carthusian house, in 1458, and served as prior in Pisa and Bologna before going to Montello, a house near Treviso in northeastern Italy, in 1467.[26] Montello, founded in 1349, had a tumultuous early history outlined by one of its monks in a chronicle in 1420.[27] Like Europe, the Carthusian order had been divided by the Great Schism, and the heads of houses siding with Rome met at Montello three times in the late fourteenth century. So Zanacchi, as fellow citizen and head of a monastery loyal to the Roman cause during the schism, was a doubly appropriate choice of holy biographer for the Roman advocate Ursulina of Parma.

Zanacchi provides exactly one date: the birth of Ursulina on May 14, 1375. Ursulina was born to Pietro de' Veneri and his wife, Bertolina. Pietro, whose family name appears in two papal bulls later granted to his daughter (and translated below), had been a widower devoted to prayer when a divine message instructed him to remarry. Several clues—not least of all Ursulina's ability to travel extensively during her short life—point to the status of this family: they were comfortable but not of the elite class of late-medieval Parma. Pietro died not long after Ursulina's birth, but Bertolina was her daughter's companion as long as she lived. Ursulina was an unusual little girl, according to Zanacchi; although she first spoke at the age of four months, she was small, unable to walk very well until she was five, and unsociable. It was at five that she began to have mystical visions, the first concerning the resurrection of the dead.

Ursulina's visions continued throughout her life. As a girl she refused to listen to sermons lest, as she explained, people might

25. The only full-length study of Ursulina to date is Ireneo Affò, *Vita della Beata Orsolina da Parma* (Parma: Reale, 1786). Affò relied on Zanacchi's account plus materials from various archives in Parma. Some of these, for example the apparently extensive transcriptions of Ursulina's visions Zanacchi describes, have not survived the intervening centuries. The brief sketch here is much enlarged by Zanacchi's full account and further explained in the notes to the translation.

26. Albert Gruys, *Cartusiana*, 3 vols. (Paris: CNRS, 1976–78), 1:174. Zanacchi subsequently returned to Parma and died as prior in Pisa in 1497.

27. *La cronaca della Certosa del Montello*, edited by Maria Luisa Crovato (Padua: Antenore, 1987).

think her holy wisdom came from them and not divine revelation. Starting when she was fifteen, at divine command she began to dictate her revelations to others, ultimately creating a great cache of writings, none of which is known to survive. Her knowledge of Scripture and theology dazzled those with whom she modestly shared it in her adolescence. On Easter, 1393,[28] the voice of God told Ursulina to prepare for a journey, subsequently specifying that she was to go to Avignon. She and her mother made the long journey, guided for a while by a figure the young visionary recognized as John the Evangelist. Once in Avignon, Ursulina received instructions to find the antipope Clement VII, with whom she spoke at length, so terrifying the prelate, as Zanacchi puts it, that he refused to see her again. Returning home to Parma, Ursulina rested only a few days before hearing a command to go to Rome and tell her story to Pope Boniface IX. When her truthfulness was confirmed by the report of a monk who had been in Avignon when Ursulina was there, she was highly honored by the pope and his court, who sent her off on a second embassy to Avignon, armed with a sealed papal letter urging the Avignon papacy and court to give up its claims to sacred authority in favor of Rome.

Returning to Avignon in early 1394, Ursulina learned of plots against her life in the Avignon court. Undeterred, she spoke so brilliantly before Clement VII and his cardinals that some of the court, in Zanacchi's account, prepared to give up its claims. But another faction remained hostile and conspired to ensure that this troublesome Italian teenager would not have further access to sympathetic ears. This group of cardinals tried (unsuccessfully) to trick Ursulina in theological discussions, accused her of witchcraft, attempted to poison her, and finally agreed to kill her slowly when an earthquake destroyed the house in which she was being tortured. The standoff continued for seven months, with Ursulina triumphant against every conspiracy and technique designed to harm her. When Clement VII learned to his surprise that she was still in Avignon, Ursulina took the opportunity to deliver the letter from Rome. Thunderstruck, he died a few days later, in September 1394. Just as the plan to reunite the Church looked as if it might succeed, the Avignon college of cardinals elected a new (anti-)pope. Her hopes dashed, Ursulina went home to Parma with her mother.

28. Because Zanacchi provides no dates beyond Ursulina's birth, those provided here derive from comparison of internal and external evidence, working forward and backward from known chronology.

A little more than a year later, Ursulina decided to go on pilgrimage to the Holy Land. For this journey, she received the express consent of the Roman pope Boniface IX when she visited Rome in early 1396; the pope's bull on the matter, addressed jointly to Ursulina and Bertolina, is also translated in this book. After an emotional visit to the holiest places in and near Jerusalem, she went home again to Parma via Venice, where she stayed briefly but left a profound memory of holiness.

The last phase of Ursulina's life began with her exile from her native city, part of a series of factional disputes in a time of civic unrest. Departing with her mother and an abbess in late 1404 or early the next year, Ursulina spent a short time in Bologna before settling for three years in Verona, where she lived in obscurity. After a painful illness relieved by many divine visions, she died, most likely in the year 1408; her feast day, that is, the presumed date of her death, is April 7th.[29]

Buried in Verona, the well-traveled visionary had one final journey; a year and a half after her death, her body was transferred to the monastery of San Quintino in her native Parma. Her cult grew across the fifteenth century, encouraged by a series of abbesses of the powerful Sanvitale family, female members of which guided the monastery for over a century starting in 1425, not too long after Ursulina reached her final resting place. The second of these Sanvitale abbesses, Magdalena, asked Simone Zanacchi to write a formal account of her life, which he completed in 1472. Miracles that had begun in Ursulina's lifetime continued through the early modern period and in 1786, Pope Pius VI declared her a saint. Her body still lies in what is now the parish church of San Quintino in Parma.[30]

From several standpoints, Zanacchi's account is typical of medieval saints' lives.[31] In one sense, that is no surprise, since

29. Affò, *Vita della Beata Orsolina*, 43–48, creates a timeline for the last years of Ursulina's life that results in a death date of 1408, rather than the traditional 1410. Affò's logic, based on Zanacchi's account, the political history of early fifteenth-century Parma, and dated documents from ecclesiastical archives, is sound.

30. We are grateful to Professor Katherine McIver of the University of Alabama for sharing her information on this church and providing us with evocative photographs of Ursulina's tomb.

31. The classic account of medieval writing about saints, first published in 1905, is Hippolyte Delehaye, *The Legends of the Saints: An Introduction to Hagiography*, trans. V. M. Crawford (Notre Dame: University of Notre Dame Press, 1961). A more recent general consideration is Thomas J. Heffernan, *Sacred Biography: Saints and Their Biographers in the Middle Ages* (New York: Oxford University Press, 1988).

he was a monk, the prior of an order of monks founded in the late eleventh century, and thus part of a long and conservative tradition; Carthusians liked to boast that their order, unlike others, had never needed reforming. The structure of the *vita* is typical, almost stereotypical. Zanacchi starts his account with great rhetorical flourish, greeting his patrons, praising the desire for an account of the holy person, saying something about his sources, and lamenting his own unworthiness, spiritual, intellectual, and stylistic, to complete the task assigned to him, asking for corrections and emendations as necessary (sections 1–2). He begins the narrative portion of the account with Ursulina's parents, both highly religious people whose holy progeny is foretold through visions and dreams (sections 3–5). Early signs of the newborn Ursulina's holiness are noted (section 5), followed by an account of her childhood and adolescence, filled with marvels concerning her physical development, visions, and humility (sections 6–11). Ursulina's first voyage comes next: her supernatural summons to Avignon, the journey there from Parma, including a stop in Provence at the shrine of Mary Magdalene, a figure much beloved by pious medieval laywomen, her reception at the papal court and conversation with Clement VII, and her eventual return home after the fearful Clement refuses to see her again (sections 12–19). Quickly following are the first journey to Rome and a meeting with Boniface IX, her second, now Roman-sanctioned journey to Avignon, where her self-confidence infuriates the papal court and where she is imprisoned and tortured and fails to prevent the election of a successor when Clement VII dies (sections 20–29). She makes second and third trips to Rome, then a pilgrimage to the Holy Land (sections 29–32). A period of holy meditation at home in Parma is ended with exile, during which Ursulina stays in Bologna, and then, for three years, in Verona (sections 33–35). During a long illness, Ursulina speaks to her companions and prays at length, begging for mercy right to the moment of her death (sections 36–40). The author proceeds with a sermon-eulogy on Ursulina's character and example (sections 41–48). After more apologies for unworthiness, Zanacchi tells about the return of Ursulina's body to Parma and then recounts several miracles at her tomb, or miracles performed in response prayers for her intercession (sections 49–56), before a brief conclusion (section 57).

Virtuous life, pious works, great devotion, a holy death, and miracles: all this is quite typical matter, set out in a standard format. Zanacchi, staying close to the hagiographical model, stresses the orthodoxy of his subject, despite her very unusual life story: Ursulina is attended to by major saints like Peter and Paul (section 5) and John the Evangelist (sections 13–16), has holy conversations throughout her life with a variety of individuals and groups on mainstream subjects like the Trinity and the nature of Jesus Christ (sections 7–40, passim), and even acts as a monastic reformer late in her life (section 35). Her final words are directed to God, prayers of praise and pleas for mercy (sections 39–40). The sermon-eulogy contains a discussion of Ursulina in relation to the seven standard Catholic virtues (sections 42–45) and stresses an eighth: chastity. The virginity lauded at the sermon's end is a kind of Christian humility, as Zanacchi explains it (sections 46–47). He refers to Ursulina as a virgin over seventy times in the *vita*, some fifteen times during her second, long visit in Avignon, as if to stress Ursulina's goodness in face of the wickedness and abusiveness of the cardinals, who try to make *her* out to be a charlatan or a witch. The miracles after her birth are equally orthodox: illnesses cured, a people in mortal peril saved, and a young woman freed from a forced marriage—by a holy illness and death on a Sunday.[32]

Finally, Zanacchi's style is as traditional as his narrative and themes. His Latin is straightforward and slightly prolix, its syntax at times more like a vernacular Romance language than its predecessor language. The Carthusian prior does not demonstrate much interest in quoting classical (pagan) authors, including authorial asides, or using classicizing vocabulary and tropes as did so many humanist hagiographers of his age.[33] That style may, however, represent a conscious choice to write in a familiar idiom rather than lack of interest or competence. Zanacchi's Montello, in fact, had some interesting literary connections. In the 1370s Montello was the beneficiary of the patronage of the noted French soldier, diplomat, crusade promoter, and author Philippe de Mézières. Around the same time, the house got

---

32. Alison Knowles Frazier, *Possible Lives: Authors and Saints in Renaissance Italy* (New York: Columbia University Press, 2005), 23–24, describes the model "canonization *vita*" as "a rigid ordering of the events of the life, followed by a survey of the virtues, then an account of the pious death and canonization, and finally a coda of miracles." Zanacchi reverses the sequence of survey of virtues and death almost completely—although it could be argued that the stress on humility and virginity woven into the biography signals those most important virtues before the account of Ursulina's death.

33. See Frazier, *Possible Lives*, 19–20 and 321 for descriptions of the style of the humanist historiographers. Most of these writers did not follow the canonization *vita* structure, either.

part of the library of a priest from nearby Padua, apparently a member of the circle of the famed poet and humanist Petrarch, others of whom were also patrons of Montello, many of them mentioned in the 1420 chronicle.[34] The chronicle mentions many books collected or copied by the monks of Montello, and in the very year Zanacchi wrote the *vita* of Ursulina, the leadership of the Carthusian order commanded four other Italian houses to return borrowed books to Montello.[35] Such tradition notwithstanding, Zanacchi at all appearances wrote with canonization of Ursulina in mind rather than humanist literary elegance and formal experimentation. But, like Raymond de Sabanac, he found his job of representing a holy woman more difficult than the apparent candor of the *vita* suggests. There are profound tensions in both these accounts of female holiness.

Women, Visions, and Politics

When Constance and Ursulina began their "political" careers, they inscribed themselves in a long tradition of women (and men) who had attempted to intervene in the politics of their time using their visionary authority.[36] From the Old Testament prophets to our fourteenth-century protagonists, visionaries throughout the centuries had relied on divine voices and revelations to guide them in their missions.[37] These missions often involved questioning established authority, warning rulers of the consequences of their misdeeds, or supporting one side in a political conflict over another. Visions and auditions of this sort were often quite different from the "cultivated" monastic visions typical of much of the mystical visionary culture of the later Middle Ages.[38] They had a direct relevance to events of the

---

34. Luigi Pesce, "Filippo di Mézières e la Certosa del Montello," *Archivio veneto* ser. 5, no. 168, vol. 134 (1990), 5–44, esp. 30–33 and documents edited at 40–44; Antonio Rigon, "Amici padovani del Petrarca e il monastero di S. Maria della Riviera," *Studi petrarcheschi* n.s. 6 (1989), 241–55 at 249–55.

35. *The Chartae of the Carthusian General Chapter: Paris, Bibliothèque Nationale MS Latin 10888, Part I, (ff. 1–157v),* ed. Michael Sargent and James Hogg (Salzburg: Institut für Anglistik und Amerikanistik, Universität Salzburg, 1985), 151.

36. See the section on "Foremothers" above for examples of Constance and Ursulina's predecessors.

37. For a brief overview see Isabel Moreira, *Dreams, Visions, and Spiritual Authority in Merovingian Gaul* (Ithaca: Cornell University Press, 2000), part I.

38. For a typology of visions and the conditions of their production see Barbara Newman, "What Did it Mean to Say 'I Saw'? The Clash between Theory and Practice in Medieval

time and often urged the visionary to some specific action. At the same time these visions often featured traditional elements centering on Christ's Passion or the Last Judgment. Constance and Ursulina both fit into these visionary patterns. Their political involvement resulted from divine commands but was complemented by visionary experiences that fit into more traditional patterns of hagiography and mystical writings.

Constance's *Revelations* move from the personal to the public rather quickly. Her first visions and auditions are concerned with her personal and spiritual life, but by 2.23 the voice begins speaking about the Count of Armagnac and his alleged treachery in seeking alliance with the English court, the enemies of France. By 2.42 the papal election of 1378 and the illegitimacy of the Avignon pope Clement VII take center stage. Constance insists repeatedly that these visions come to her unbidden but that nonetheless they must be revealed to a larger public (3.4). She is aware that these visions will cause her serious problems, especially with the clerical establishment in Toulouse. In a letter (3.3) she describes how the divine voice articulated the problems resulting from her visionary activity and her outspokenness. Constance's eventual imprisonment and disappearance eloquently testify to the risks she ran by becoming a political visionary.

Ursulina's case is quite different. Zanacchi wrote the *vita* long after her death, with a view to her canonization. Thus the first account of visions we find in the *vita* is a set piece of hagiography: her parents learn of their daughter's future birth and destiny through angels. At age nine Ursulina begins to share her visions and revelations with others. It is significant that the first vision recounted in any detail (sections 11–12) is the one in which the Lord tells her to go to Avignon and rebuke the antipope Clement VII. Thus Zanacchi explicitly links Ursulina's visionary experience to her political mission. Further commands for Ursulina's diplomatic shuttle mission between the popes of Avignon and Rome are not uttered by a divine voice but come straight from the Roman pope Boniface IX, an important contrast with Constance's long series of orders given her by the divine voice. Unlike Constance, Ursulina has no visions of popes and cardinals burning in hell nor is her own spiritual life a subject for intense visionary experiences, at least within the framework of the *vita*.

Raymond de Sabanac and Simone Zanacchi thus show us two different ways of integrating visions and politics. Raymond transcribes

Constance's visions as they happen; the text is not very tightly structured and shows his confusion and misgivings when faced with the visionary outbursts of this passionately engaged woman. Simone's carefully organized text highlights one of Ursulina's visionary experiences, the one that legitimizes her future actions. Both women were divinely inspired to work for an end of the Great Schism but neither of them succeeded: like the Old Testament prophets, who could serve as their models, they were finally no more than two of the many voices crying in the wilderness of a Church rent in two.

Because we know so much more about Ursulina's biography, though, we can speculate from Zanacchi's account that the tiny saint's involvement in the high drama of pan-European ecclesiastical politics had an echo at home in Italy.[39] Zanacchi provides a few tantalizing hints of his subject's place in local and regional politics. The overlord of Parma in Ursulina's early years was Gian Galeazzo Visconti, the duke of Milan.[40] After her second journeys to Avignon and Parma, Ursulina goes "at divine command" to meet the duke, who first scorns her but is ultimately won over; Ursulina commends him in particular to "the defense of the Catholic faith," that is, the Roman papal cause, and tells him not to interfere in matters of religious dogma (section 29). The precise nature of Ursulina's concerns, expressed before her departure for the Holy Land in 1396, is not clear, but entanglement in local politics is evident in the series of events resulting in the exile during which she died. The dominion of the Visconti over Parma was interrupted by the death of Duke Gian Galeazzo in 1402. The main factions vying for control of the city were led by Ottobono Terzi and Pietro Rossi, with Ottobono seizing control in 1404. Zanacchi reports that he summoned Bertolina, Ursulina's mother, and told her to get out of town before a candle placed by the town bell burned down. The

39. See Luongo, *Saintly Politics* for a thorough discussion of the involvement of one saint, Catherine of Siena, in the complexities of Italian affairs; the remarks that follow are much indebted to Luongo's insistence on the importance of female religiosity in "the assumed male and secular cultural ground of late-medieval and Renaissance politics" (22). Alison Frazier argues that the production of a hagiographical compendium called the *Sanctuarium*, published in Milan ca. 1477, was in part politically motivated (*Possible Lives*, 101–67, passim).

40. On the political history of Parma in this era, see Bernini, *Storia di Parma*, 83–92; a more detailed account of the early fifteenth-century scene is Marco Gentile, *Terra e Poteri: Parma e il Parmense nel ducato visconteo all'inizio del Quattrocento* (Milan: Unicopli, 2001). We rely on both in the paragraphs that follow.

party of exiles included Abbess Maristella of San Paolo, who was at Ursulina's side when she died (sections 34–35, 37).

There was apparently more to the story than what Zanacchi describes as exile, in the company of a local abbess, at the hands of a tyrant who was annoyed at Ursulina's peaceful meditative retirement in Parma. Earlier, the prior named "the great armor-bearer and commander" Gherardo Aldighieri as one of Ursulina's scribes (section 9). Gherardo stands out from the list of scholarly and clerical scribes: he was a condottiere, a successful soldier of fortune and indeed one of Parma's most famous soldiers. He had joined the party of Pietro Rossi but was captured and killed by the forces of Ottobono in 1403. Ottobono also attacked the nunneries of San Paolo and San Quintino,[41] suggesting that religion played a part in his strategy for domination. The departure of an abbess along with Ursulina and Bertolina was more than flight from aggression aimed at her house. Abbess Maristella was a member of the Aldighieri family, possibly Gherardo's sister;[42] she had first fled Parma, along with some of her community, into the safekeeping of Rossi allies.[43]

From these scraps of information, a few possibilities emerge. It is clear that Ursulina was involved in politics at least enough to advise the duke of Milan and suffer exile as a member of the party opposed to Ottobono. But Ursulina may have been more important than that. Zanacchi provides no details about Ursulina's activities between her return from the Holy Land and her exile from Parma, a period of eight or nine years. We might wonder if, in that period, her fame— Zanacchi's accounts of her holy work in Urbino, Venice, Bologna, and Verona suggests her company and advice were often sought out— made her a spiritual guide or protector for some of Parma's powerful families, like those in other cities perpetually feuding and fighting in a complex series of alliances. Ursulina, it would appear, was strongly linked to the Aldighieri clan and, whether previously or subsequently is impossible to guess, to Pietro Rossi. When Ottobono told Bertolina to leave Parma, he may have wanted to further the spiritual aspect of

41. Marzio Dall'Acqua, "Il Monastero di San Paolo," in *Il Monastero di San Paolo*, ed. Dall'Acqua (Parma: Franco Maria Ricci, 1990), 24 and, on San Quintino, Italo Dall'Aglio, *La Diocesi di Parma*, 2 vols. (Parma: Scuola Tipografica Benedettina, 1966), 1:180.

42. Affò, *Vita della Beata Orsolina*, 40–43 and notes, which reproduce contemporary documents referring to "domne Maristelle de Adhigheriis abbatisse monasterii Sancti Pauli Parmensis."

43. Dall'Acqua, "Il Monastero di San Paolo," 24.

his campaign by removing a religious figure hostile to his interests—and was perhaps intimidated enough by her reputation to give the order to her mother instead of the fearless Ursulina.

Such a position of political importance also adds a new dimension to the return of Ursulina's body to Parma. If she died in 1408, as is most likely,[44] then the homecoming a year and a half later would have come on the heels of the assassination of Ottobono in 1409. The return of Ursulina was part of a normalization of affairs after the brief dominion of Ottobono (whose enemies mutilated his body). It was also an element in the revival of the monastery of San Quintino, also the target of Ottobono's wrath, its goods taken and its inhabitants expelled. Although Visconti influence over Parma was restored, the Rossi family thrived in the fifteenth century, even amid changes of overlordship.[45] In death, then, Ursulina was not only a holy visionary but also, we propose, a symbol of the restoration of political and religious order in early fifteenth-century Parma. Finally, it is even possible that Zanacchi's reluctance to relate Ursulina's visions had some political motivation. Duke Galezzo Maria Sforza succeeded his father as duke of Milan in 1466, and his insouciance led to renewed struggles for influence in Parma among four families, two of whom were the Rossi, the former allies of Ursulina's scribe Gherardo Aldighieri, and the Sanvitale, of whom Zanacchi's patron Abbess Magdalena of San Quintino was a member. Factional troubles were still abroad when Zanacchi completed his commission in 1472; only a few years earlier a local writer had written that there was no love or charity in Parma and that cruelty reigned there.[46] Maybe Zanacchi (who was from Parma, after all) thought it wiser not to give detailed accounts of heavenly revelations dictated to the one-time ally of a faction that was, as he wrote, at odds with the family of his patron abbess. Like Raymond de Sabanac, Zanacchi found his job of representing a holy woman more difficult than the apparent candor of the *vita* suggests. And there are even more profound tensions in both these accounts of female holiness.

---

44. See above, note 29.

45. Bernini, *Storia di Parma*, 85–95, passim. Maristella's difficulties on her return to San Paolo probably explain why Ursulina's body was not taken there; another abbess had been elected in her absence and a long legal battle to regain her office ensued (Affo, *Vita della Beata Orsolina*, 41, n1).

46. Bernini, *Storia di Parma*, 92.

Difficult Subjects, Reluctant Authors

The complex relationship between holy women and their male confessors and/or biographers has been the subject of a number of fascinating recent studies.[47] The dynamics between these "couples" varied. Sometimes the male cleric exercised the function of censor but also of a publicizer of a woman's visions, as was the case for the Benedictine nun Elisabeth of Schönau (1129–1165) and her brother Ekbert. Sometimes the male cleric observed, admired, and befriended the holy woman as did the Swede Peter of Dacia with the German Christina of Stommeln (1242–1313). But frequently an entirely different image of the woman emerged from her own writings than from the texts authored by the male clerics. Thus while Peter emphasized Christina's role as bride of Christ in his writings about her, in her own letters she highlighted the "vexations" caused by demons and the bizarre physical sufferings she was subjected to for years. Another striking example is Catherine of Siena (1347–80) who, in the hundreds of letters she dictated, showed herself a forceful, politically engaged woman. But in the life composed after her death by the great Dominican Raymond of Capua, she is portrayed above all as a mystic whose most important trait was her intimate connection with Christ. This life was meant as the first step in a planned canonization process and therefore elided Catherine's activism and sometimes unorthodox behavior.[48]

In almost all cases involving the pairing of female visionary and male cleric we find a "two-sphere model" of authority: through her visions and revelations the woman had a more direct access to the divine but lacked the institutional authority of the male cleric; the male cleric possessed ecclesiastical credentials but could not muster the charismatic powers of the visionary. Or, as John Coakley puts it succinctly, "she had what he needed."[49] The reverse, of course, is also true.

47. *Gendered Voices: Medieval Saints and Their Interpreters*, ed. Catherine M. Mooney (Philadelphia: University of Pennsylvania Press, 1999); Jodi Bilinkoff, *Related Lives: Confessors and Their Female Penitents* (Ithaca: Cornell University Press, 2005); John W. Coakley, *Women, Men, and Spiritual Power: Female Saints and Their Male Collaborators* (New York: Columbia University Press, 2006).

48. On these three couples see the essays by Anne L. Clark, John Coakley, and Karen Scott in *Gendered Voices*, ed. Mooney and Coakley, *Women*, chaps. 2, 5 and 9; on Catherine's political roles see Luongo, *Saintly Politics*.

49. Coakley, *Women*, 216 and 22.

For an understanding of the relationship between Constance and her confessor, Raymond de Sabanac, the sources are much more limited than for, say, Christina of Stommeln and Peter of Dacia or Catherine of Siena and Raymond of Capua. We have no biographical data on Constance and we do not know how the two met nor how they parted. Constance left just a few independent writings in the form of letters, but not enough to allow us to differentiate her voice clearly from that of Raymond de Sabanac.

From the preface on the discernment of spirits we can deduce that one of Raymond's preoccupations was Constance's orthodoxy. He assures his readers—who are not identified in any way—that Constance's virtues place her in the realm of orthodoxy and that therefore one must believe her visions. Unlike some confessors/ biographers, such as Raymond of Capua or John of Marienwerder, the confessor of Dorothea of Montau (1347–1394), Raymond de Sabanac is not a major character in his own transcription of Constance's revelations. He does seem to make a distinction between the "I" that participates in the action and the "I" that writes when he says "...*her confessor* reproached her with two things; one *I* will leave aside, as for the other one *he* said to her..." (2.43; emphasis added), but on the whole his role is that of the reluctant scribe.

Most of the instances where he refers to himself indicate that he was wary of Constance's visions (since they contradicted the prevailing church policies of his area) and that only his conviction of her holiness made him write at all. Indeed, at least once he received an official missive forbidding him to write down Constance's visions (2.20). On the other hand, the "voice," which is Constance's interlocutor, assures him of eternal glory if he keeps on writing (2.34). At various points Raymond is so unsure of his mission that he asks for a divine sign to tell him whether to go on writing or not—and which he promptly receives in the form of an illness (2.22). Although in some ways the reluctance to write which is then overcome by divine command is a literary trope designed to allay readers' skepticism, Raymond's case has an additional element that is absent from most stories involving holy women and cautious biographers: he ran a distinct political risk in continuing to transcribe Constance's dangerous and controversial revelations. Thus throughout the *Revelations* there seems to be a tug-of-war between Raymond's urge to obey what he sees as a divine command to write and his fear of the ecclesiastical authorities.

This tug-of-war finds its clearest expression in one of Constance's letters, a text that we assume gives us a more direct access to Constance's voice. Here she writes about a vision of Pierre de la Barrière (d. 1383), the bishop of Autun she detested, being tormented in hell: "And I told my confessor, but he told me to reject this vision for he told me it was untrue" (4.4). But the vision returns nonetheless and the divine voice reassures her that it is true "no matter what your confessor says" (4.4). This kind of direct conflict is absent from Raymond's own writings and gives us a glimpse of the kind of debates that must have occurred between these two rather frequently, given the riskiness of Constance's visions.

Raymond and Constance thus form a couple of forceful visionary and reluctant scribe whose relationship finally remains unresolved, since Constance disappears from the stage in an unknown manner. Her imprisonment and ultimate disappearance also explain why there was no follow-up to this text: no canonization proceedings could be initiated for a woman who used her visionary powers to denounce the very prelates who would have to support her case.

Ursulina of Parma and Simone Zanacchi make a rather different sort of couple. Zanacchi's knowledge of his subject was entirely secondhand. In that sense the pair had no relationship; of more immediate importance was Zanacchi's relationship with his patrons, the community of nuns at San Quintino, who clearly hoped to promote the cult of the woman whose relics were housed in their church. Around 1450, the community had written to city leaders asking for money. The body of Ursulina, they explained, had done many miracles in Parma and also in Venice, where there was a project to build a monastery in her honor. In fame lay danger: the nuns feared that unless a secure chapel were built, the holy body might be taken away—which disaster would bring shame on the monastery, the city, and its citizens alike.[50] It is not clear exactly what the results of this plea were, but Abbess Magdalena Sanvitale, elected in 1456, built a new cloister and commissioned Zanacchi to write the *vita*.

Despite its straightforward appearance, some strains are apparent in what Zanacchi produced. The prior seems uncomfortable with the visionary, mystic aspects of his subject's religiosity. He is vague about the exact nature of her experiences and goes into very little

---

50. The document is printed in Affò, *Vita della Beata Orsolina*, 69–70. In section 32 of the *vita*, Zanacchi states that Ursulina's holy behavior during a stay in Venice after her pilgrimage to the Holy Land was still remembered at the time he wrote.

detail about them, especially given the great amount of material he says he has at his disposal, including seven transcribers of her visions, one of whom set down "several volumes" (see sections 1 and 9). He buries a lone mention of levitation during visions in a relative clause in the middle of the narrative of Ursulina's exile from Parma (section 35). Instead, Zanacchi is at pains to reassure readers, implicitly and explicitly, that these visions were authentic; much like Raymond de Sabanac, he stresses orthodoxy as a proof of credibility. The question of discernment of spirits that Raymond addressed directly clearly worried Ursulina's biographer, a manager-monk.[51]

Zanacchi spends much more time recounting Ursulina's travels and travails, especially in Avignon. In this lively narration, divine inspiration seems to cause less worry, and can explain Ursulina's learning and her courage in the face of hostile male ecclesiastics. Discussion of Ursulina as traveler and pilgrim puts her squarely in the mainstream of late-medieval holy women. At divine command, Ursulina transformed herself into a frequent traveler. In her first long trip, by foot from Parma to Avignon, Ursulina and her mother meet a mysterious pilgrim who turns out to be Saint John the Evangelist, echoing the experience of Bona of Pisa (d. 1207), who acquired Saint James as a travel companion.[52] Once Ursulina is finished with her papal shuttle diplomacy, she still cannot bear to sit at home. In 1396 she decides to go on a pilgrimage to the Holy Land. Women had become pilgrims to Jerusalem as early as the fourth century; Margery Kempe (c. 1373–after 1438), provided a lively account of her problem-laden pilgrimage in her autobiography. Among the late-medieval female Jerusalem pilgrims the most famous was probably Birgitta of Sweden (1303–73) who, prepared for more than thirty years by visions predicting this trip,[53] set out for the Holy Land in November 1371. She and her companions were almost killed in a shipwreck. Birgitta

---

51. Newman, "What Did it Mean to Say 'I Saw'?"

52. For remarks on the risks of travel and the necessity of male escorts for Bona and Ursulina see Diana Webb, *Medieval European Pilgrimage, c. 700–c. 1500* (New York: Palgrave, 2002), 92. Norbert Ohler calculates that a traveler on foot could cover 15–25 miles a day (the trip from Parma to Avignon is over 400 miles). Fourteenth-century papal express messengers on horseback could hope to cover 60 miles a day (on level ground). See *The Medieval Traveller*, trans. Caroline Hillier (Woodbridge: Boydell, 1995), 101.

53. Both Birgitta and Margery had visions that announced and legitimized their trips. See Kristine T. Utterback, "The Vision Becomes Reality: Medieval Women Pilgrims to the Holy Land," in *Pilgrims and Travelers to the Holy Land*, ed. Bryan F. Le Beau and Menachem Mor, (Omaha: Creighton University Press, 1996), 159–68.

then spent four months visiting holy places, accompanied by many visions that intensified her experience.[54] In line with late-medieval focus on the corporeal aspects of devotion, Zanacchi emphasizes Ursulina's emotional and physical response to the places of Christ's birth, suffering, and death. Even after her return home, Ursulina continues her meditations by reliving her experiences with sobs, sighs, and groans (section 33). Zanacchi treats Ursulina's pilgrimage as a manifestation of her inner life, a proof of her intense devotion to Christ's passion in one mode characteristic of late-medieval pilgrimage accounts. Ursulina's journey is depicted as an occasion for prayer and meditation, not as a chance to see new people and places, a central theme in many contemporary pilgrimage accounts.[55]

Looming large over the story of Ursulina is the figure of Catherine of Siena, a touchstone for many female holy women of the late Middle Ages, who was both an activist and a mystic. Catherine died when Ursulina was a girl and had been canonized in 1461, only eleven years before Zanacchi penned his account.[56] The *vita* stresses its subject's multifarious actions in the world—her embassies to Avignon, her pilgrimages to the shrine of Mary Magdalene and the Holy Land—but also the special privileges awarded to her by the pope, her sensual experiences and subsequent meditations on the places of the Passion, her refusal to listen to preachers, and her deathbed confession not to a priest but to Christ himself. Zanacchi even goes so far as to address Ursulina as his mother (section 42). In this mingling of spheres, Catherine is very much a model, but Zanacchi does not choose, as Catherine of Siena's biographer Raymond of Capua did, to favor the aspect of her religious life he found discomfiting. Nor does he surround Ursulina with male admirers or devotees: of eight miracles recounted, only two are for the benefit of men and in both cases the intercessor was a woman (in one case a sick boy's mother).

54. See Aron Andersson, *St. Birgitta and the Holy Land* (Stockholm: The Museum of National Antiquities, 1973).

55. For narratives that stress the touristic and exotic, see Nicole Chareyron, *Pilgrims to Jerusalem in the Middle Ages*, trans. W. Donald Wilson (New York: Columbia University Press, 2005). A general account is Jonathan Sumption, *Pilgrimage: An Image of Mediaeval Religion* (Totowa, NJ: Rowman and Littlefield, 1975).

56. There is yet another connection: the early history of Montello, Zanacchi's house, was intertwined with the activities of Catherine of Siena's followers in Venice and the Veneto. See Donato Gallo, "Dalla Certosa del Montello alla Certosa de Vedana: La Fortuna dei certosini nell'ambiente veneto del Tre-Quattrocento" in *La Certosa di Vedana*, ed. L. S. Magoga and F. Marin (Florence: Olschki, 1998), 14–15.

Raymond of Capua's Catherine is surrounded by admiring men who support her efforts at reform; Zanacchi names only Boniface IX as a male advocate, and the accounts of meeting with him are far less detailed and vivid than those with members of the papal court at Avignon. The prior's account is no slavish imitation of the work of Raymond of Capua, or, to put it another way, he cannot or will not make Ursulina adhere to that model.

In his sermon-eulogy, Zanacchi, through emphasis on humility and virginity, labors to make Ursulina, an odd peripatetic laywoman, into a model for nuns. Again, the picture does not fit into the frame. The miracle story Zanacchi develops most fully—it is three times longer than any other account—is a very traditional tale of a chaste woman whom Ursulina helps to escape forced marriage by holy virgin death. Perhaps Zanacchi wished his subject was so easy to portray in standard hagiographical format. The nuns of San Quintino, who stressed Ursulina's many divine visions and revelations in their letter of ca. 1450, may have found Zanacchi's account ultimately unsatisfactory. Ursulina emerges neither as a full-blown quasi- or para-monastic charismatic or mystic, nor as the kind of female lay "living saint" popular in the period, characterized by care for the poor, sick, and downtrodden, teaching, fasting, and other bodily discipline, and spiritual gifts including both mystic raptures and somatic manifestations of holiness, like stigmata.[57] Abbess Anna Sanvitale, who succeeded her aunt Magdalena in 1483, did manage to erect a new marble tomb for Ursulina in 1507, but the hoped-for canonization was delayed almost another 300 years.[58] Perhaps this was due in part to the nature of Zanacchi's *vita* and its somewhat confused, even schizophrenic attitude toward its subject, a tiny, energetic, fearless, and devout female mystic, pilgrim, and ambassador.

Note on the Texts and Translations

The Revelations of Constance de Rabastens were translated from the Catalan by Renate Blumenfeld-Kosinski from the edition by Amédée Pagès and Noël Valois in *Annales du Midi* 8 (1896): 241–78, based on the unique manuscript, Bibliothèque nationale de France, ms. lat. 5055. She also consulted this manuscript for her translation. Con-

---

57. See Zarri, "Living Saints."

58. Such a delay is hardly unique. The formal canonization process for Clare of Montefalco began shortly after her death in 1308 but papal approval did not come until 1881.

stance's text occupies folios 35 recto to 58 recto in a miscellany of Latin texts. It is the only vernacular piece in the entire manuscript. It bears the title *Revelationes Constantiae de Rabastens quae vivebat anno MCCCLXXXIV cum aliquot litteris eiusdem ad Inquisitorem fidei* (the Revelations of Constance de Rabastens who lived in 1384 with some of her letters to the Inquisitor of the faith). This title was written in the seventeenth century by Etienne Baluze (1630–1718), a famous historian of the Avignon papacy.[59] However, Baluze does not mention Constance in his works.

The manuscript is made up of many texts from different periods and in different formats. A number of the folios are torn and resewn; other folios have been torn out and only remnants remain near the binding. Several folios are bound upside down. A number of texts, such as Josephus's *History of the Jews*, stop in mid-sentence. The codex also contains some mathematical drawings as well as an image of Noah's ark with mathematical notations. In other words, the codex has no theme or logical sequence of texts. One set of folios (140–51) dates from a more modern period, possibly the seventeenth century. It is impossible to know who put this manuscript together and whether there was any rationale behind this heterogeneous collection.

The folios containing Constance's *Revelations* are evenly trimmed and look rather clean compared to the rest of the manuscript. The text was written by two distinct hands that alternate at irregular intervals. One hand looks to be more rapid and energetic as well as less careful. The other hand is much more carefully done. Other features include an empty space for the initial D at the beginning of the text (fol. 35r) and a little cross that someone drew over the word "creu" (cross) on folio 52v.

The transcriber of Constance's visions, Raymond de Sabanac, hailed from Toulouse. He wrote down Constance's visions in either Provençal or, most likely, in Latin. That text is lost. The fact that the *Revelations* were translated early on into Catalan shows that at least one (anonymous) author considered them important enough for his or her region to render them into the local language.

The modern French translation by J.-P. Hiver-Bérenguier, *Constance de Rabastens: Mystique de Dieu ou de Gaston Fébus* (Toulouse: Privat, 1984), 173–206, contains too many errors to be useful.

---

59. See Valois and Pagès, "Les Révélations de Constance de Rabastens et le Schisme d'Occident (1384–86)," 241.

Bruce L. Venarde was primarily responsible for the translation of Simone Zanacchi's Latin Life of Ursulina of Parma. The text is *Acta sanctorum quotquot toto orbe coluntur*, 68 volumes (Antwerp, 1634–1940; reprinted Brussels, 1965–70), April, volume 1, 723–39 (first published 1675). As the editor, the Jesuit scholar Daniel Papebrochius, explains, the nuns of San Quintino in Parma, where Ursulina's body was preserved, had the Latin biography translated into Italian and published in 1615. This being the only version of Zanacchi's account available, Papebrochius translated it into Latin and was ready to publish it in the *Acta Sanctorum* series when, at the last moment, the nuns discovered a manuscript containing Zanacchi's original Latin version. It is this text that he reproduced in the volume cited above. No copies of the Italian translation seem to have survived, nor has the multivolume description of Ursulina's visions that Papebrochius states existed in the mid-fifteenth century, housed by the nuns of San Quintino and the Carthusian monks of Parma. The Latin manuscript from which Papebrochius worked had apparently disappeared again by the time Ireneo Affò wrote his sketch of Ursulina's life in 1786 to celebrate her canonization, since he worked from the *Acta sanctorum*. The scholars we have consulted in Italy have found no trace of a manuscript of Zanacchi's Latin text, nor of the numerous Latin and vernacular texts on which Zanacchi claims it drew, and that Affò says still survived in part in 1786. Venarde also translated the two papal bulls addressed to Ursulina (120–22, below) from Latin texts in Affò, *Vita della Beata Orsolina*, 65–68.

The editors reviewed and improved each other's translations.

The Revelations *of Constance de Rabastens*
by Raymond de Sabanac

Part 1: Preface[1]

The Holy Fathers and the Doctors of the Church say that a person who has visions must be examined in such a manner that one can know whether she is a spiritual person or whether she is worldly or secular; whether she lives under discipline and in special, perpetual, and spiritual obedience to some saint or aged father, discreet, mature, virtuous, Catholic, and proven; or whether she lives according to her own will and desire. And further, whether she has submitted the temptations and the visions that contain them to the examination and judgment of her spiritual father or other aged spiritual fathers, with humility, all the while afraid of being led astray or deceived; or whether she has hidden some visions and not submitted them to anyone's examination and judgment; or whether, based on [these visions] she has perhaps arrogated to herself some vanity or vainglory; or whether she shows disdain toward others. And it must also be examined if this person who has these visions follows them by true and virtuous acts of obedience, humility, charity, and steadfastness, or rather by acts of concern for her reputation, of boasting, and of arrogance, of display and a growing appetite for human praise, a neglect of prayers or a desire for honors and dignities. And further one should examine whether this person has a reputation among people of being a true Catholic, faithful and obedient; and whether she has persevered with humility in having visions for a long time or whether she is a novice and persevering; and whether the person having these visions has a good and true natural and spiritual understanding; and whether she has discreet judgment in reason and spirit or whether she has flighty judgment, with too much imagination or fantasy. For

---

1. The chapter divisions reproduce the layout of the edition by Pagès and Valois, which follows that of the manuscript (BnF lat. 5055, fols. 35r-58r) although in the manuscript the sections are not numbered. This preface articulates succinctly the doctrine of the discernment of spirits. See the Introduction for details and bibliography. For a commentary on this preface see R. Blumenfeld-Kosinski, "Constance de Rabastens and the Discernment of Spirits," in *Medieval Christianity in Practice*, ed. Miri Rubin (Princeton: Princeton University Press, 2009), 290–95. Generally on the discernment of spirits see Caciola, *Discerning Spirits* and Elliott, *Proving Woman*.

Saint Gregory says in his book the *Dialogues* that saintly men can distinguish by intuition and by the voice of their hearts whether visions showing the same images are illusions or revelations, and for this reason they know what is sent by a good spirit and what by a bad spirit.[2] And one has to know whether this person will be examined at other times concerning the merit and circumstances of her visions by knowledgeable, literate, spiritual, and experienced men or not. All these things must be considered during the examination of this person.

As for the manner of seeing or hearing spiritually and of receiving revelations and visions, the Holy Fathers and Doctors of Holy Church say that one must examine with great subtlety whether this person who has seen visions and has heard words was awake or asleep or dreaming, and whether she had a corporeal, imaginative, or spiritual vision, or whether this was by chance an intellectual supernatural vision; and whether in a new mental ravishment called ecstasy, that is, an elevation of her thoughts, she has seen or felt things that come from divine love or not ... [words missing in manuscript]; or whether she has seen any mysteries speaking of spiritual ... [words missing]; or in which species or semblance these persons see things, and whether they feel an illumination or the enlightenment of supernatural intelligence and a manifestation of divine truth.

Concerning things seen or not seen, the quality of the person and the subject matter of these visions, it has to be examined whether these visions accord with the Holy Scriptures or whether they disagree with or contradict them; and whether these visions are a delight for humans leading to virtuous actions and the salvation of souls or whether they lead to error in the Catholic faith; and also whether they demonstrate anything monstrous or superfluous in nature or new, and whether they lead to anything which does not agree with or is beyond reason; or whether they keep us away from good, virtuous, and humble deeds; and whether these visions are always true or sometimes false and lying, that is, one has to know whether these things sometimes reveal themselves to be true and sometimes false and mendacious, and whether they indicate to us future honors, riches, and human praise or humility in all things, or whether they

---

2. Gregory the Great, *Dialogues* IV.50: "Sancti autem uiri inter inlusiones atque reuelationes ipsas uisionum uoces aut imagines quodam intimo sapore discernunt, ut sciant uel quid a bono spiritu percipiant, uel quid ab inlusione patiantur." Ed. Adalbert de Vogüé, trans. Paul Antin, 3 vols. (Paris: Cerf, 1978–80), 3: 174–76.

rather lead us to an exaltation of arrogance ... [words missing]. . ... and we are admonished to obey the pure, spiritual persons ... and our superior prelates.

For reasons of brevity I finally say that perfection in this matter comes from the quality of the visionary and from the quality and manner of seeing, and also from the quality and manner of the visions and from the manner of knowing the spirits shown, inspired, and manifested by these visions; and whether these are good or bad spirits will be demonstrated in this Book of Revelations.

For without such a subtle examination made beforehand, a dangerous error could ensue if we were to approve or censure the person who sees visions of these things or revelations without reflection or with abrupt haste. If by chance a hasty, indiscreet, and thoughtless person, given to fantasies, would approve of such a visionary and her visions, then she would receive false things as true and would perilously reject the true as false, and thus the good and true visions and divine pronouncements would be disdained. They would not be believed and go unheeded[3]... . [passages missing in manuscript]. And even today such error occurs because of a lack of a discreet and careful examination. So, all these above-mentioned matters that we have considered in theory are visible in the things she has seen and in the quality of this person, that is, in this spouse of Christ, the blessed Constance from the place called Rabastens in the county of Toulouse. It would be suitable to recount her life in order to demonstrate the truth of all the above-mentioned points, for her reputation would thus be manifest in all the world. But I lack the skill to do this. Rather, the marvelous visions contained in this book which our lord God has revealed to her will clearly tell of and demonstrate her virtues, for her life and her noble deeds and the explanation of all this would take too long to recount. If, however, it becomes necessary that such a particular book should circulate, it will appear at that time.[4]

3. This is an important point. Most often theologians stressed the danger of being deceived by demonic visions but Raymond also highlights the opposite danger here: not accepting true visions for fear of demonic deception.

4. Perhaps Raymond is thinking of a moment when someone might promote Constance's canonization, in which case a Latin *vita* would be called for.

Part 2

1.

It all started when she was asleep in her bed one night and she had a vision of a hillside on which there was a multitude of dead people. And a voice said to her: "You should know that there will be a great mortality, but be strong and fear nothing that you may see or hear." A short time later her husband died.

2.

One night, after her husband's death, she was reflecting on her life which she thought she had spent badly as far as God was concerned; and she was thinking how she could serve God well, and how she could make up for all these past times when she fell asleep. And a voice told her: "Do not have any doubts, for you should know that you will place your children well and that you will leave the world behind."

3.

Another time she meditated on the Passion of Jesus Christ and desired to feel the pains that he had borne for us in her body and suddenly she felt a great pain in her left arm. She fell asleep and a voice told her: "Do not fear, you will be healed."

4.

Another time around midnight she meditated how at this same time of night the son of God had been bound to the pillar. Then she knelt down in prayer and felt suddenly that someone was pulling on her right arm; and she felt such great pain that she thought she could never be cured of it. And she suffered such great pain that she could not sleep or find any relief, neither during the day nor the night. But one day she fell asleep and a voice said to her: "Ask me whatever you wish." And she answered: "Some relief and the salvation of my soul." And she felt that her arm was being stretched and when she woke up she felt greatly relieved. But she had not slept longer than it takes to say three Paternosters, for her confessor, briefly absent, had had barely enough time leave the room and return quickly to her.

5.

The third night after that, she could not pray as was her custom and complained to God, saying "Oh, my Lord God, do not abandon me!"

And around […] she fell asleep and she had a vision of a man dressed in satin who said to her: "You should know that I am the one you have in your heart […], now you see me." And then he disappeared and she no longer saw him. He said: "Now you do not see me but you should know that I am always beside you, so do not ever again say: 'Lord, you have abandoned me.' Know that I have not left you and that I will never leave you, and that I pray to my father for you."

6.

Likewise, another night when she could not entreat God nor pray with great devotion nor even say her prayers, she complained to God. And toward dawn she fell asleep and heard a voice that said to her: "Do not fear, for your soul is in better condition than it was before, for your heart was in pain and did penance."

7.

Another time, one night after compline she was praying in her oratory and a black demon in the form of a cat appeared to her[5]; it was moving in front of her and all around her and bared its teeth as if it wanted to bite her. But in spite of all this she continued her prayer.

8.

Another night after matins when she had said her prayers she fell asleep and saw two ships. In one of them there were many people, but there was no one to guide it and it was sinking. In the other one there was just herself and two other people, and the ship was skirting danger but a voice said not to be afraid, and it arrived in the harbor and was safe.

---

5. Compline is one of the "Hours": they are matins, lauds, prime, terce, sext, none, vespers, and compline, moments of the day set aside for recitation and contemplation. See John Harthan, *The Book of Hours* (New York: Thomas Y. Crowell, 1977). Starting around midnight and spaced at about three-hour intervals, the times assigned to the Hours are variable, depending on the season and other factors. These prayers were monastic in origin but by the later Middle Ages they were also often performed by pious lay people. The cat was often considered demonic and was also associated with heretics and witches who were thought to use cats in their ceremonies. For a striking image of the devil as a cat (being worshipped by heretics) see Wolfgang Behringer, "How Waldensians became Witches: Heretics and Their Journey to the Other World," in *Communicating with the Spirits*, ed. Gábor Klaniczay and Eva Pócs (Budapest and New York: CEU Press, 2005), 159.

9.

Another night after she had said her prayers she fell asleep and had a vision of a young man who showed her a coffer filled with great splendors but which was rotten, old, and worn on the outside. He said to her: "Your body is just like this; outside it is ugly and worn out from penances but on the inside it is filled with great virtues." Right away she thought this was an illusion and turned to God saying: "Dear God, by your mercy, protect me from any illusion and deception by the demon."[6]

10.

On another day she went to the Friars Minor[7] and there was one devout friar who was afraid of her, since he had taken a vow of chastity and everything was still new to him; for which reason he told her that she had acted badly and that perhaps this time she would err but not recognize it, and he said many other things like this. Because of this she left very distressed, and the following night, after compline, she went up to her oratory and prayed to God crying copiously and asked Him to please protect her by His mercy.[8] Then she fell asleep and in a vision she saw six paupers who said to her: "Know that we are angels and that God has sent us to comfort you; do not be afraid but be certain that you will never err." And she had endured great torments of

6. Constance's body is thus the opposite of whitewashed sepulcher of Matthew 23:27, which is beautiful on the outside but inside full of "dead men's bones and uncleanness." This scene also shows that Constance fits the criteria of the discernment of spirits that Raymond laid out in the preface. Her humility makes her doubt the vision of the young man and appeal to God for guidance.

7. The term Friars Minor designates the Franciscans, the religious order founded by Saint Francis (1182–1226).

8. Weeping copiously is a sign of piety that became particularly popular with Marie d'Oignies (1177–1213) whose life was written by James of Vitry. In the fifteenth century Margery Kempe, an English woman who tried to imitate pious models like Marie, also wept constantly. On the spiritual background of this kind of behavior see Piroska Nagy, *Le don des larmes au Moyen Age. Un instrument spirituel en quête d'institution (Ve–XIIIe siècle)* (Paris: Albin Michel, 2000). See also Geneviève Hasenohr, "*Lacrymae pondera vocis habent.* Typologie des larmes dans la littérature de spiritualité française des XIII-XVe siècles," *Le Moyen Français* 37 (1997), 45–63. Hasenohr shows that in the later Middle Ages the initially monastic ideal of shedding devotional and contritional tears was adapted for the laity through many pious treatises in the vernacular.

sexual feelings for thirteen months, but after this moment she did not feel them any more than if she were dead.[9]

11.

Another day she heard mass from her confessor and after the Paternoster she prayed to God saying: "Lord, give me a lesson, teach me what I should ask for." And she had a vision and a voice said to her: "Ask that wisdom may guide your words, your steps, and your glance."

12.

On another day her confessor was chanting mass and when he elevated our Lord[10] she adored a little cross that was part of her rosary and some inspiration spoke to her spirit: "Kiss your hand so that you remember that you are dust and will return to dust. And henceforth wear this cross." And she did as she was told.

13.

Starting on another night when the sky was a deep red and everything seemed to be on fire, she prayed for three days and three nights while weeping copiously. And after matins when she had said her prayers she fell asleep and had a vision of a naked man who was covered only by a white cloak. His right side and arm were uncovered as was his head, and he held in his hand a large wooden cross and he was standing on a high hill. The hill and its sides as well as a great valley below were all filled with countless people. And on top of this hill there was a platform and the man stood in the middle with herself beside him and the man said: "I command that the earth open up and that those damned by my Father enter there." And then the earth trembled and all cried loudly: "Jesus Christ, have mercy on us." And no one entered [the earth]. And then the man said: "I command that the heavens open and that my Father descend with all the saints." And then everyone cried: "Lord, keep your word and descend immediately." But she saw nothing else.[11]

---

9. This encounter with the frightened Franciscan seems to signal the death of Constance's sexual self.

10. I.e., the Eucharist.

11. This vision of the Last Judgment is rather inconclusive. No one seems to be condemned to hell, but Constance does not see everyone enter heaven either. In medieval paintings usually roughly equal numbers of people descend into hell and are led to heaven. See for

14.

One day she was praying in her house and meditated on God. She fell asleep and heard a horrible and frightening trumpeting, very loud and high pitched, which made her think of the Last Judgment and she was terrified and trembled greatly. And the voice said: "Do not be afraid, for you should desire this day. When you see the heavens open, or when the heavens are open and you see this blessed glory, you should rejoice greatly as you think about this vision."

15.

Another time she was very ill and around compline she still had not said the none prayer. She began to pray and when she had finished, her body began a great debate with her soul. The body said: "I will never be able to bear so many things." And the soul answered: "Body, do not be bothersome, but obey the soul, for if you do this a great crown will be your reward." And this debate went on for a long time. After midnight, when she had said her prayers, she was trembling so hard that her body was all shaken and dissolved. She fell asleep and saw in a vision a man dressed like an Augustinian brother who said to her: "Look to the heavens." And as she did so she saw a sky of fire and the fire fell on the earth and burnt people, and everyone fled and hid in caves, and this man said to her: "Be careful not to turn back, but go forward."[12] And she responded: "Lord, I will never turn back for anything but I will tell my daughter that we all have to honor our vows."

16.

Once, for two and a half days she had a great desire to see Our Lord and the second night around midnight she was asleep with this desire and then woke up and meditated on her life and her failings. She realized that at one point she had not trodden the road of God's commandments. She said: "Lord, I thought that I desired to see you. I realize that I am not worthy of thinking about you nor of seeing you." She felt great pain and sadness over her failings and in this sadness she fell asleep and saw the heavens open. There was a tree so green

---

example the Last Judgment in the early fourteenth-century Cloisters Apocalypse or Roger van der Weyden's "Last Judgment" in the Hôtel Dieu in Beaune (1443).

12. This passage seems to be an allusion to Sodom and Lot's wife who was transformed into a pillar of salt when she turned around to look at her burning hometown. See Genesis 19.

that she had never seen nor heard described such greenness.[13] And it was all covered with big round fruits like apples, so white and shining that no one could take the measure of them and there was a cloud immeasurably more resplendent than the sun and on this cloud there were about twenty-four ancient men who walked two by two as in a procession. And in this cloud you could hear many voices like those of children chanting melodies so pleasant and gracious that no one could ever describe them.

17.

In 1384 when there was an earthquake around the feast of Pentecost, she fell asleep one night after having said her prayers and saw in a vision the heavens full of a great multitude of birds which looked like swans, and the bodies of these birds were more resplendent than the sun. The wings were made of gold and their entire bodies were covered with round discs like the Host, but the color was like the azure from India, and they kept their wings spread out. She asked: "What is this?" And the voice, which was that of a man, answered: "These are angels and you should know that soon you will see great signs." And suddenly a cloud covered the birds and the next year there appeared great penury, mortality, and famine.

18.

Another time she was so troubled that she could not find respite; she went into her room and began to pray to the Holy Trinity and she resolved to do this for a long time. And suddenly she had a vision in her heart of the heavens open and there was a cloud so resplendent and bright that no one could describe it, and she was much frightened by this vision. And the voice said to her: "Take the Book of Revelation and see what it says." The next day she asked her confessor whether there was a book called the "Book of Revelation" and he answered:

---

13. The tree is a common motif in mystical thought. See Roland Maisonneuve, "L'expérience mystique et visionnaire de Marguerite d'Oingt," in *Kartäusermystik und -Mystiker*, ed. James Hogg (Salzburg: Institut für Anglistik und Amerikanistik, Universität Salzburg, 1981), 81–102. On greenness (*viriditas*) and its associations with Paradise see Peter Dronke, "Tradition and Innovation in Mediaeval Western Colour Imagery," *Eranos Jahrbuch* 41 (1972), 51–107, esp. 82–88.

"Here it is, my lady." And he had her read it but the words that she heard astonished and frightened her greatly.[14]

19.

Once she meditated for two days and two nights, almost against her will, on the Holy Trinity and prayed to God while weeping copiously, motivated by the fear of meditating too much.[15] She said: "Lord, by your mercy protect me from any error and do not permit that I meditate on such things, for I am not worthy." And she fell asleep and around dawn she saw in a vision a marvelous lord who was high up; from him descended a column like a resplendent ray of sunlight and the lord was on the upper capital of this column. On the lower capital there was another lord and in the middle a third one was encased so that he was visible inside. They were swathed in white garments and were all alike, except the one on top who seemed larger and who told her: "See here the Holy Trinity: this is the Father, this is the Son, and this one here is the Holy Spirit. But do not believe that in heaven this looks exactly the way it looks here.[16] But the love that springs forth from them is so great that one calls it the Holy Spirit." And she said: "Lord, may it please you by your mercy that if this is a diabolical illusion, you make it immediately disappear. But if it comes from you, may honor and glory be given to you, for I am not worthy of seeing such things, although I do believe firmly in everything Holy Church believes in."

20.

On January 13 she went to Toulouse in order to hear mass celebrated by her son Amangau who was a monk at [the monastery of] La Daurade and who was going to say mass the following Sunday. And she wanted to keep all these things secret and she asked the inquisitor[17]

14. This passage tells us much about Constance's lack of education since she was not aware of the existence of the Book of Revelation. As for her reading, the Catalan text reads "E feu los legir," which could also mean that Raymond pored over the book with her and read it to her.

15. One gets the impression here that perhaps Raymond cautioned her against excess in her meditations. This would be in line with the French theologian Jean Gerson's (1363–1429) somewhat later writings warning against any excesses in lay piety. Constance's ensuing vision of course invalidates such warnings!

16. An interesting note of caution against a too literal interpretation of this type of vision.

17. Hugues de Verdun was the inquisitor at Toulouse at that time. The inquisitor was both prosecutor and chief justice—"a conflation that was extremely prejudicial to the defendants." See Elliott, *Proving Woman*, 127.

and her confessor, Raymond de Sabanac, to advise her whether these things came from God or from a demon, for she did not want to reveal them unless she had their permission and that of the holy council of the Church and of the clergy. They held a general council and other more specialized ones concerning these things that had been disseminated in the town and in other places. Henceforth neither she nor her confessor would be permitted to write down or reveal [her visions]. This was decided by a letter from master P. Guillem de Luc from the chapel of the lord archbishop of Toulouse, on the last day of the aforementioned month.[18]

21.

Every day things like the ones described above happened to her, or even more. But her confessor did not want to write them down because he wanted to obey his superior. And the voice told her: "Tell your confessor to write down these things for they are truly from God; tell him that he must obey God more than human beings." In spite of all this he did not want to write, for he was afraid of offending God and his superior unless God should give him some sign or miracle. And every day he prayed that God might give him some sign whether he should write or that he might give him some illness and that no one should be punished but he alone. And around mid-October he fell very ill and his illness lasted until mid-May and on Easter Sunday people even feared he might die.

22.

On May 8 when she got up around midnight to say her prayers she was enraptured. And the voice said to her: "Tell your father [confessor] to remember the things he has asked me for, namely that he asked for a sign whether he should write. I gave him such an illness that no human being will be able to cure him; only I can, the true God. Write the things that I reveal to you, for it is necessary for the people that you write them down. And he should be more obedient to me who is the true God than to the world or to the serpent full of malice that thinks all day about where to spit its poison. It can be compared to the

18. This happened in 1385. See Valois and Pagès, "Les Révélations de Constance de Rabastens," 243. Jean de Cardailhac (d. 1390), bishop of Rodez and patriarch of Alexandria, had been appointed to the archbishopric of Toulouse by Pope Urban VI in July 1378 but changed his allegiance to Clement VII several months after Clement's election. See Noël Valois, *La France et le Grand Schisme d'Occident*, 4 vols. (Paris: A. Picard: 1896-1902), 1:117 and 2:403.

viper which, once it has conceived, can only give birth by dying.[19] This is what will happen to him, he will die an eternal death. In no other time were there as many evils as there are at present: the faithful will obey the infidels and the faith will be as nothing." And she said: "Oh my Lord, there was no greater evil than when your creatures died." And the voice responded: "Those who were persecuted will be reborn from death to life."

23.

On the same day of that month which was a Monday she heard mass in the chapel of Saint-Jean, and after the elevation of the host she was enraptured and the voice said to her:[20] "The letter dealing with the betrayal that you must send to Toulouse: write it from beginning to end and put in it—exactly as you saw—how the election was made of the just man who is the true pope and tell how you saw that I transmitted to them the Holy Spirit.[21] And they saw it but did not recognize it, for they were unworthy. Rather, in this very place they complained against me and spread the fallacious errors that Pierre de la Barrière has sown and they exalt them.[22] For as long as these errors are not eradicated there will no peace in the kingdom of France. Flanders is being destroyed and they prepare to move against the young tree."[23]

19. The viper was reputed to split open and die when giving birth. See Lynn Thorndike, *A History of Magic and Experimental Science*, 8 vols. (New York: Columbia University Press, 1923–58), 1:172.

20. Elevation is the part of the liturgy of the mass when, according to Catholic doctrine, the bread is transformed into the body of Christ. The Catalan word for "enraptured" is *raubida*, which designates a kind of spiritual "ravishment" where the body becomes unimportant.

21. The "them" of this sentence probably refers to the cardinals who elected Pope Urban VI in April 1378. This is the first indication of Constance's political mission: to buttress the legitimacy of the Roman pope Urban VI.

22. The bishop of Autun, Pierre de la Barrière (d. 1383), had refused an appointment as cardinal from Pope Urban VI in 1378 but then accepted one from Clement VII a few months later. In 1379 he had written, for the French king Charles V, a treatise in favor of Pope Clement, refuting Giovanni de Legnano's pro-Urban *De fletu Ecclesiae* (On the tears of the church). For an even sharper condemnation of this bishop see below Letter 4. See Valois, *La France et le Grand Schisme*, 1:131.

23. For the complicated situation in Flanders see the introduction. The "young tree" is the French king Charles VI.

24.

Another time during high mass she was enraptured and the voice said to her: "Take pity on the people and do not fear to denounce treachery, for you should know that the count of Armagnac delivered his seal to them[24] and that the king of England believes everything they say. Thus the treachery is sealed and confirmed." And she saw this three times. And she was also told to transmit all this immediately to Paris.[25]

25.

At compline in the chapel of Saint-Jacques[26] she was in doubt concerning the things she had learned on the subject of the treachery and she prayed to Our Lord that he protect her from illusion and that no one should be deceived by her. And she was enraptured and the voice told her: "Do not have any doubts, for I tell you that the count of Armagnac can be compared to Pontius Pilate who, when he was governor of Jerusalem, did not recognize me, his true God, although he was right there in Jerusalem." She breathed deeply and rejected this vision.[27]

26.

Another time on a Tuesday at midnight when she got up to say her prayers, she prayed to God that he protect her from any demonic illusion, as she had done earlier, with many tears and pains. She was enraptured and the voice told her: "Do not have any doubts, for I tell you that I am the true God and wherever you go I will be with you." And she said: "Lord, I know that the true God is in heaven and on earth and everywhere. Wherever I may be, you will be there too." And the voice told her: "Do not have any doubts but persevere, for before the world was created I had chosen you to reveal these things. And I

24. It is not quite clear who this "them" (*ells* in the Catalan) refers to; it may simply refer to the English.

25. For this rather confused paragraph see the Introduction, 22.

26. See fig. 11 in Hiver-Bérenguier, *Constance de Rabastens* for a photo of this chapel, which is part of the church Notre-Dame du Bourg in Rabastens. The chapel and its paintings date from 1318–20. See Hiver-Bérenguier, 86. The Web site for the town of Rabastens speaks of "an explosion of color" for the frescoes of this chapel, which seems to indicate a periodic freshening of the colors.

27. The voice seems to imply that it should be easier to recognize the true God if one is closer to holy places like Jerusalem. This vision is the first to be explicitly rejected by Constance, though Raymond does not tell us why.

told you that the count [of Armagnac] can be compared to Pilate who, when he was governor of Jerusalem, did not recognize me, who am the true God, and did not recognize the Lord from whom Jerusalem springs. And I tell you that when the count comes to rule he will not recognize me nor the young tree, that is, the king of France, and he will destroy him and the French kingdom, and more if he can. Then will rise up the crane with the vermilion head,[28] that is the count of Foix, who will lift up the just man, that is, the Roman pope and will put him on his throne. And in the same way that Vespasian came to destroy Pilate[29] the count of Foix will come and destroy [the count of Armagnac]. And he will dominate the realm and there will be such a great union between the king of France and the count of Foix that the king will obey the count in many things. And after that the count will accept the command of the Holy Passage [crusade][30] in order to avenge my death, I who am the true God." And she said: "How can it be that you reveal these things to me since I am a vile sinner full of shame and vileness?" And the voice answered: "Do not have any doubts. Cry out in a loud voice, for the time has come for you to reveal my secrets." And she had this vision three times.

27.

And before she began to write this she was enraptured and the voice said: "Do not be afraid to name the count [of Armagnac] for he is the tyrant who wants to destroy the kingdom, if he can."

28. Cranes were believed to represent "Christian foresight and wisdom" and, by extension, wise rulers in the Middle Ages. See Beryl Rowland, *Birds with Human Souls: A Guide to Bird Symbolism* (Knoxville: University of Tennessee Press, 1978), 33. The color red may be linked to Gaston Febus's association with Apollo and the sun.

29. Vespasian was Roman emperor from 69–79 CE. The conflict between Vespasian and Pilate is the subject of a group of very popular French texts generally known as the *Vengeance de Nostre-Seigneur* (The vengeance of Our Lord). Based on apocryphal gospels, such as the *Death of Pilate*, these texts were reworked throughout the Middle Ages. They tell the legend of Veronica and her veil as well as the story of the destruction of Jerusalem by Vespasian and his son Titus (70 CE). At the end, lengthy passages tell of the horrible execution of Pilate. See for example *La Vengeance de Nostre-Seigneur*, ed. Alvin E. Ford (Toronto: Pontifical Institute of Mediaeval Studies, 1984).

30. The crusade was a preoccupation of many people at this time, including saintly figures like Catherine of Siena (1347–80). On the crusades in the later Middle Ages see Norman Housley, *The Later Crusades, 1274–1580: From Lyons to Alcazar* (Oxford: Oxford University Press, 1992).

28.

On the day of Pentecost at the hour of compline she was praying in the chapel of Saint-Jacques when the voice told her: "You should know that at this moment some of the people that interrogated you are assembling, for they want to know who are the ones who committed treason. Do not be afraid to cry out loud and denounce the treachery, for you should know that Bernard of Armagnac and his brother have renounced me and my power and have taken the devil as their lord and that they will give all the support and help they can to the king of England against the young tree and the king of England will do the same for them." This happened to her three times.

29.

Another time she went to the council in Rabastens and told them not to conclude a treaty with the count [of Armagnac] for the reasons described in the preceding chapter. Another time, in the year of Our Lord 1384 at the beginning of March, she said it again: " My lords, take care to note when someone tells you that a truce was declared between the kings of France and England, for you should know that this will be treachery, as I have written above." And she said many other things that were not written down, but they did not pay attention and great tribulations followed until finally they recognized that she spoke the truth. On the Saturday after Pentecost some people came to her and asked her to pray to Our Lord for them that he might teach them how to govern themselves. She answered: "Lords, I advise you to correct [your behavior] and that you turn back to Our Lord and also to implore the chaplains[31] and the poor people in whatever way you can." And while praying she told them the various ways in which they had committed great sins.

30.

On Sunday May 22,[32] after she had confessed, she was praying in the chapel of Saint-Jacques. She prayed to Our Lord very devoutly that he might take pity on the people just as he had on the Magdalene and on the robber [Lk 7:2 and 23:39–43]. And she also said many other words that would take too long to transcribe about how they should comport themselves to God's honor. And this prayer followed on the

31. The Catalan text says *capellans*, probably as a synonym for priest. Churches are called "chapels" in the text for the most part.

32. May 22 was a Sunday in 1384.

Saturday when the [the counselors of Rabastens] had spoken with her. The following night while praying she was enraptured and remained in ecstasy all through high mass. The voice told her: "You will speak to them of the inhabitants of the city of Nineveh that was to perish but because they converted I revoked the sentence. If someone is afflicted with a serious illness, one looks for the best physician to cure this illness. These people who complain against me and my followers are afflicted by a grave illness and I am the physician who heals both the body and the soul. I am not like the other kings who desire vengeance when they have been offended and I do not want vengeance, but I want them to convert. For it is useless for them to try to protect themselves unless I protect them. When a city is well guarded and there is great artillery or barbicans it is safer. And I promise you that if they convert and do the things I want them to do, for your sake I will surround them with moats, and these moats will be my angels, and the artillery will be the Holy Spirit that will defend them."

31.

On the feast day of Saint Bartholomew [August 24], which was a Wednesday, a great lord, a baron from the Bordelais region, came to see her. He told her that some Saracens had arrived to ask certain officials of the king of France to show them a mountain in which was hidden a great treasure together with many other jewels and two casks of balsam. And they said that they only wanted the balsam and that the rest would be for the king of France. The lord baron said to this woman: "Why don't you pray to God to find out what to do and if it pleases God to tell everything secretly to the king of France?" The next day, a Thursday, before compline, she prayed to Our Lord and she was enraptured and the voice told her: "Do not be afraid to say anything, cry it out loud, for you are the one who has to announce the coming of the Antichrist. You should know that the Saracens are Antichrist's disciples and that they want to open the Sacred Treasure to the detriment of the people.[33] And they want the balsam that heals and fortifies

---

33. "Saracen" is a medieval term for Muslims. It is not clear what kind of event Constance refers to here. The view of Saracens as disciples of the Antichrist was widespread in the Middle Ages. See Richard K. Emmerson, *Antichrist in the Middle Ages: A Study of Medieval Apocalypticism, Art, and Literature* (Seattle: University of Washington Press, 1981), 67–68; John V. Tolan, *Saracens: Islam in the Medieval European Imagination* (New York: Columbia University Press, 2002), esp. 45–50; and David Burr, "Antichrist and Islam in Medieval Franciscan Exegesis," in *Medieval Christian Perceptions of Islam: A Book of Essays*, ed. John V. Tolan (New York: Garland, 1996), 131–52.

so that it will heal and fortify them so that they can conquer God's people." And on this day and the next she had this vision five times.

32.

On many other occasions the voice revealed the following things to her: "Go and tell the archbishop of Toulouse to look up in the Book of Revelation the passage where John says that a trumpet will sound in seven cathedral churches announcing the misfortune to come [see Rev 1:10-11] and that the words of Daniel have been fulfilled: "When you see in a holy place the establishment of desolation and abomination, let him who reads it understand it, for we are close to misfortune" [see Dan 9:21-27]. And this is what is happening in the heart of the college [of cardinals] in Avignon, for this is the temple where I should dwell but the words have been fulfilled: 'False prophets will rise up' [Mt 24:11]. These are the cardinals of Avignon who compare themselves to me and claim to incarnate the truth, but they have sown false errors throughout the world."

She breathed deeply and said: "Lord, by the mercy that you had for your people when you drew them out of Pharaoh's power, and by the pity you had on our father Adam, who through his disobedience merited eternal damnation, but whom you liberated from limbo to transport him to eternal glory, may you revoke the judgment of the college of Avignon." And she was enraptured and the voice said: "If Abraham had prayed in the same way for the city of Lot [see Gen 19] it would not have perished."

She breathed deeply again and said: "Lord, just as you are alone I am alone, and I do not ask for counsel from any human but only from you. May it please you not to destroy the creatures that you have made; but the pains that they must endure, give to me, provided they are not eternal, and may it please you to teach me how they should comport themselves." And she was enraptured and the voice told her: "There are few who want to drink from my chalice, but those who will drink from it I will protect and defend, and there is no one who should be greater than this Lord, but there are many who want to be with the destroyer of the faith rather than with me the eternal God. There are many who want to know when the tribulations will end but no one has a right to know except I the eternal God."

And she breathed deeply and said: "May it please you by your holy mercy to wish to reveal these things to some holy creature, but I am a great sinner and not worthy of being believed." And she was enraptured and the voice told her: "These things can be known only through a miracle, and it is a great miracle that it is you who will proclaim the Holy Scriptures to them for you are ignorant of them. But he who has ears will hear." And every time the voice told her that she should write down these things, but they were only written down on the next to last day of September because her confessor did not want to write them down.

33.

On Tuesday, the fourth of October, after midnight when she had said her prayers, she was enraptured and the voice said: "Write down the seven seals of which speaks the Book of Revelation [Rev 5:1], for the first is the Holy Divinity; the second is any human creature who cannot recognize the Divinity's great humility when it was incarnated; the third is the Incarnation; the fourth is that no one is worthy of opening this seal except I, the son of God; the fifth will be opened by a woman; the sixth is that you will be this woman; the seventh is now opened." She breathed deeply and said while meditating in her heart: "Lord, I am not worthy of these things. Lord, John already saw these things, why did he not proclaim them?" She was enraptured and the voice said: "It was not yet time. It is one thing to open the book but another to proclaim my secrets."

She breathed deeply and rejected this vision but she was again enraptured and the voice said: "Be not afraid, for I want you to write because many false religious people glossed these seven seals erroneously." She breathed deeply and said: "Lord, do not show me these things for I am not worthy; rather show them to some holy creature who is worthy, for if I speak of them myself no one will believe me." She was again in ecstasy and the voice said: "Do not doubt, for the Holy Scriptures will bear witness to you and you will bear witness to me and the deeds that I have done but will not do again in days to come." And she saw this vision five times during this night. She had had this vision continuously for two years, but she did not want to write it down because she did not understand it well.

34.

On a Wednesday the voice told her: "Tell your father [confessor] that he should feel no embarrassment at writing these things, for a good workman when he has begun a good work is only satisfied when it is finished. Tell him also that he should not resent the work of writing, for when the work is finished great glory awaits him, from the beginning of the world and without end. Nothing in the world will be able to deprive him of it."

35.

On a Thursday after midnight when she was up in order to say her prayers, she prayed to the Lord that he should give her a sign whether it would please him if she transmitted these things to the council just as they had been said above. And she was enraptured and the voice said: "Do not be afraid to transmit them, for the good worker must show his good work so that people will praise God the Father" [see Mt 5:16].

She breathed deeply and rejected this vision but again she was in ecstasy and the voice told her: "Do not doubt these things for the destroyer of the faith wants to destroy those who are commanded to my service." After her prayers she returned to her bed and was immediately enraptured and saw a great lord with great power, glory, and magnificence on a throne. At his feet there was a beautiful white lamb holding in front of it a book sealed with seven seals. Suddenly it transformed itself into a man and showed her one seal after the other saying: "The first is the Holy Divinity; the second is any human creature who cannot recognize the Divinity's great humility when it was incarnated; the third is the Incarnation; the fourth is that no one is worthy of opening this seal except I, the son of God; the fifth will be opened by a woman; the sixth is that you will be this woman; the seventh is now opened." And he said to her: "Open the book." And she was afraid to touch the book for he had said that no one was worthy of opening this book except he himself. But he said to her: "Do not be afraid to open the book." And she opened it and it was all written in gold, outside and inside, and the seals were of gold as well. She said: "Lord, I see the book but I do not know the letters." And the voice said: "Do not be afraid, for here is written what I and the prophets have proclaimed, and I am that true God of whom John spoke who came to make the mute speak, and the time has come when the Son of Man will show his power."

36.

On a Saturday when she heard mass in the chapel of Saint-Jean she still had doubts about the abovementioned vision, and when the priest donned his liturgical vestments she fell into ecstasy again after the elevation, and the voice told her: "Do not have doubts about this vision but look at the book." And she looked at the book again and had the same vision as described above.

37.

On the Saturday which was the third day of October around midnight, after she had said her prayers she was enraptured. And the voice said to her: "Write in red letters that the world will last only another seven years and that in seven years the kingdom of France will suffer a great blow and will be laid low, for it supports the pope of Avignon.[34] And transmit this message to the royal council in Toulouse so that they will transmit it to Paris." And she had this vision more than twenty times.

38.

On the following Sunday she listened to a mass celebrated by a Friar Minor in a hostel called Verlhac.[35] After the elevation she was enraptured and the voice told her: "It is now time that the work you have begun should be made public and do not be afraid, for you should know that just as I have suffered tribulations for the whole world, you will suffer tribulations for the whole world, and in these tribulations my power will be shown. But know that just as the Holy Divinity does not leave my body, I will never leave you and know also that it is time for the Son of Man to show his power." And many other things were said that are not written here.

39.

On the night of All Saints' Day at matins she was enraptured and the voice said to her: "Write down the vision that John speaks of in the Book of Revelation, the one where he says that he saw a multitude of people speaking different languages [Rev 7:9]." After matins she breathed deeply and rejected all these things, but after confession she was enraptured and the voice told her: "Be not afraid to write since it is necessary that you write, for John's vision signifies that you will see many people who speak different languages, and there will be some who will try to excuse themselves by saying that they would gladly

34. This prediction was later interpreted as announcing the madness of the French king Charles VI that began in 1392.

35. The Catalan *hostal* may refer to a place where mass was celebrated, although it was not a church, perhaps a resting place on the pilgrimage route to Compostela that traversed this region.

preach the Scriptures but that no one would understand them. Therefore the testimony you will bear against them in the coming days will
be all the stronger because you will understand them all, and so they
will not be able to excuse themselves anymore."

40.

Indeed, some churchmen threatened some people that they would
withhold the Holy Sacrament from them and would cause all kinds of
trouble for them. The next day, the day before All Saints' Day, before
going to sleep she prayed for them, and she was enraptured and the
voice told her: "Tell them not to be afraid but to remain strong, for
there will be many scandals, and they must come. For those who love
me there will be an increase in glory, but for evil people there will be
an increase in pain. And misfortune will strike those who cause the
scandals." This happened on a Wednesday.

41.

The next day, Thursday morning, when she was in the chapel of Saint-
Jean, she was enraptured and the voice said to her: "Oh, such a great
misfortune will arrive, and when it comes everyone will want to know
the truth of the things you say, and you will be interrogated, and the
dragon will come to devour you. But you will be given wings and you
will be transported into the desert,[36] and after the desolation of the
Church, Antichrist will arrive."[37]

42.

On Monday, November 6, around midnight, after her prayers she was
thinking about how the queen of Naples died and why she had to die
in this manner.[38] And she was enraptured and the voice said to her:
"Tell the bishop of Albi that the queen was measured with the same
measure that she herself had used.[39] And tell him that there is no one
who can deceive me, who am the true God. They will be deceived

---

36. Like the "woman clothed in the sun" in the Book of Revelation, Constance will thus be
protected from the apocalyptic dragon (see Rev 12:14).

37. In the Middle Ages there were several different schemes predicting Antichrist's arrival.
Most common was the idea that Antichrist would arrive as a counterfeit Christ and wreak
havoc in a period before the Last Judgment. See Emmerson, *Antichrist in the Middle Ages.*

38. Queen Joanna of Naples died in prison in the summer of 1382. For details see the introduction and Valois, *La France et le Grand Schisme,* 2:8–51.

39. Joanna had been suspected of engineering the murder of her first husband.

themselves and they know well that the election of the Avignon pope was made against my will and was falsified, and that they too will be measured by the measure they have used. For the red beast will rise up, that is, the Roman pope of whom John had spoke in his Book of Revelation, and red signifies the fire of justice with which he will destroy them."[40]

She breathed deeply and said: "My Lord, you told me that just as you had suffered tribulations for the whole world, I would suffer for the whole world. May you erase them from the book of my life and may you forgive them." And she was in ecstasy again and the voice said: "Tell the bishop of Albi that I remind him of the example of David: for even if Saul persecuted him he did not want his death [see 1 Sm 23-26]. And I tell you that even though they have persecuted me I do not want their death. And transmit the message to him that he should not hesitate to tell the truth out of fear of death, for I am the true God and will protect and defend him. I am not Antichrist like the other kings who want vengeance when they are offended. I do not want vengeance but only that they may convert themselves and live."

43.

On Tuesday evening her confessor reproached her with two things; one I will leave aside, as for the other one he said to her: "Lady, one could say that when you asked to be deleted from the book of life or that God should forgive them, you said something unjust and contrary to what you said earlier, namely that you wanted to suffer pains for them, provided these were not eternal. To be deleted from the book of life would mean eternal damnation." That same day she heard mass and prayed to Our Lord with great devotion that she should not ask for nor say anything that might be unjust or disagreeable to him, and that if she had done anything like that that he might forgive her. And she was enraptured and the voice told her: "Do not doubt that this is just, for Moses said the same prayer.[41] But yours is even stronger, for Moses prayed only for the people he led but you pray for the entire world. And believe that I forgive them, not because of your merits

---

40. It is surprising that this vision equates her beloved Roman pope with Saint John's red beast of Revelation 12:3 since a few verses later John explicitly identifies the red dragon as "Devil and Satan" (Rev 12:9). The identification is repeated in 2.45.

41. This passage is a slightly garbled allusion to Exodus 32:33 where Moses prays to the Lord to "blot [him] out of the book of life" if the Lord cannot forgive Moses' people's sin of having made a golden calf for a blasphemous act of worship.

but by my mercy. And if a king had a knight who risked death for the honor of his king, it would be very bad for the king not to defend or protect him. I am the king for whom you risk death and for this reason I will defend and protect you, for it is time that the work you have begun should be known."

44.

People told her that some highly placed people called her crazy. This evening before going to sleep she began to pray, weeping, and asked God for forgiveness. She was enraptured and the voice told her: "Why do you doubt that these things will happen?" And then she felt very strongly that all the torments that one could describe were inflicted upon her because of these doubts. And the voice told her: "Do not have these doubts, for when the world was made it was decided by the Holy Trinity that these things should happen. And remember the things that you have heard and seen, for I tell you that just as you have seen that my mother was abandoned by every human creature at the moment of my Passion [see Jn 19:25] so you will be abandoned, but my power will never abandon you." And she breathed deeply and said: "Lord, you know that my soul and my body are ready to do your will."

45.

Another day a clerk sent her a formal inquiry on whether the situation of the Church was advantageous and whether my lord the duke of Anjou was dead.[42] She began to pray and said: "My Lord, you told me how you are all alone and I am also all alone. May it please you to tell me which answer I should give them, for I do not know where to turn except to you." And she was enraptured and the voice told her: "You will answer that he is dead who carried the sign of the beast, that is, the duke of Anjou. As for the Church, tell them that the time of the evil beast has arrived of whom John had spoken in his Book of Revelation where he saw a red beast, that is, the Roman pope. And the evil beast will not be so well hidden in the close that it cannot be found."

46.

On November 6 a sealed letter was presented to her from a great lord, but no one could tell where it came from, and the man who carried

---

42. Louis, duke of Anjou (1339–84), a brother of the French king Charles V, was regent during Charles VI's (1368–1422) minority and had hoped to obtain the kingdom of Naples with the help of Clement VII.

it could not or did not want to say. Here are the things that were in the letter: the person who sent it suffered from a serious illness that he had had from the day of his birth until today, that is, for more than sixty years. He wanted to know what she thought of the state of the Church and in which one of the two elected men [the popes] one should believe, and whether the Schism would last a long time and when the war between the kings [the Hundred Years' War between England and France] would come to an end.

And she answered that she did not meddle in things like this nor did she care about them. In the evening during dinner she got a headache and she was enraptured and the voice told her: "The one who sent you this letter is the archbishop of Narbonne, who sent it in order to deceive you. But he will be the one to be deceived. Do not be afraid to respond that his illness is grave, but that it will not last forever. And do not believe what he wants you to believe, for his illness has not lasted sixty years, in fact, not even ten. As for how long the Schism will last, no one is authorized to know the time it will last, except for me the eternal God. For the bad it will last not long enough, and for the good it will last too long. As for the war between the kings, say that the kingdom of France will not be free from tribulations until the bad weeds that are planted in the fields have been torn out and thrown away. And as for the question on whom to believe tell him that through woman the faith was preserved and through a man it will be revealed. And because he has written to you in such an obscure manner I want you to respond to him just as obscurely."

47.

On the last day of November a priest came to her and alleged that he had seen some writings telling him that the end of the world was near. After compline she was praying in the chapel of Saint-Jacques and she was enraptured and the voice told her: "They can realize very well that the end is near, for the ages are past, and at that time the entire world will be disturbed; and at this moment there is trouble throughout the world and all the elements are disturbed and tremble. Because of all this they can recognize that the time is near when the Son of Man will judge them from the highest heavens."

48.

On the thirteenth of January in the year of Our Lord 1385, which was a Wednesday,[43] she was praying after midnight. And she was enraptured and saw a temple filled with smoke and darkness, and the Avignon pope was inside. And above him there was an angel holding a naked and bloody sword as if he wanted to kill the pope. And then she saw four men holding ampoules in their hands, and a voice said: "Take the seven vials and give them to seven angels who will pour them out over the entire world, for it is time that the Son of Man show his power" (see Rev 16). And she said: "May it please you to reveal these things to some holy creature, but I am a great sinner and not worthy of being believed, nor would anyone believe me." And the voice responded: "John spoke of a trumpet. You have denounced in seven cathedral churches the false errors and the false betrayals that were sown in my name.[44] And the Holy Scriptures will bear witness on your behalf." And she thought that when the voice said vials that it actually said ribbons.[45] And the voice told her: "Vials are containers or ampoules which are full of maledictions, and there are many people who believe that this is already over, but they are deceived. And I tell you that heaven and earth and everything else will pass away, and these things will turn out to be true. Write all this down."

49.

On Thursday the abovementioned maledictions were shown and explained to her, but it would take too long to describe them here and just about all of them are contained in the Book of Revelation, chapter sixteen, but nonetheless she described some more.

50.

On Friday again, when she heard mass, she was enraptured several times and was shown the vision of the ampoules described above, and the voice told her: "Write down the things you have seen and cry out to the archbishops and prelates about the humiliation that is prepared for the unfortunate ones." And she answered: "My Lord, no one wants

43. January 13 was actually a Friday in 1385. It is possible that Raymond recalls the date incorrectly or else the Catalan translator made a mistake. January 13 was a Wednesday in 1384.

44. See above, 2.32.

45. It seems that Constance understood the word "fiales" (vials) as the word "fil" (thread) which in the Catalan is *pany de rauba*.

to believe me; rather, they say that I have a demon in my body." And the voice answered: "Remember the things I told you, namely that almost all the things I have endured you will endure. And they also said of me that I had a demon in my body [see Mt 12:22; Lk 11:15]. Tell the prelates and priests who have the spirit of prophecy that these things must be revealed. He who has ears will hear."

51.

Toward the end of January, one night after her prayers she was enraptured and had a vision of a lord who distributed throughout the earth many treasures and various jewels. But the lord had leprosy and many people accepted his treasures and jewels, but those who took them became as leprous as this lord as soon as they had taken them.[46] And she was told by Our Lord God: "Know that the lord you saw stands for the Avignon pope; leprosy signifies simony; the leprous people stand for those who accept benefices through simony, and those who give them are just as leprous as those who accept them."[47]

52.

On the evening before Easter Day, around midnight after her prayers she was enraptured and she saw three ships: two of them were well equipped with fortifications and towers, but no one steered them and they were in deep waters. And on the shore there was a great multitude of people, men and women of all sorts, and this woman [i.e., Constance] screamed loudly: "Do not board these ships, for they are full of demons." Then she was approaching the shore, and the ship she was on was not equipped like the others, but in much poorer shape. And a limping man left the other men and boarded this ship and immediately he and the ship sank to the bottom of the sea, and for a long time it seemed as if the water was boiling at this spot.[48]

She marveled at this vision and the next day, which was Easter, she was enraptured when she was in church. The voice told her: "The two well-equipped ships you saw signify the world which is proud of its vainglory, but no one steers it. The ship that arrived on the shore is the Church which cries for pity. The limping man who boarded it

46. On the moral connotations of leprosy in the Middle Ages see Saul Brody, *The Disease of the Soul: Leprosy in Medieval Literature* (Ithaca: Cornell University Press, 1974).

47. Simony is the securing of ecclesiastical positions through payment, in Christian thought an especially heinous sin because it was regarded as purchase of spiritual authority.

48. Constance says nothing about where she was in her vision when this third ship sank.

is the Avignon pope and he will have no pity on the Church but will destroy it if he can.[49] But you should know that the Church will pass through great dangers but will not perish. He, however, will be thrown into hell." And all these things were shown to her several times and even more often when she was told that she was to be interrogated, which gave her the courage to confront her interrogators.

53.

On Monday, April 13th, after compline she was praying in the chapel of Saint-Jacques and she was enraptured and the voice told her: "You should know that many rumors will swirl around you because of false witnesses that accuse you, but do not be afraid, for the betrayer of the faith who compares himself to me and who wants to be lord of the entire world, that is, the Avignon pope, will perish in one instant. For just as the ship which he boarded perished the moment he entered it, he will immediately perish in hell. And do not have any doubts nor seek any human counsel for you will receive none, but divine help will never abandon you." And she breathed deeply and said: "O Lord, how can all this happen to me who am such a sinner!" And the voice responded: "Do not be afraid, for I tell that the time has come for the Son of Man to show his power, and it will be shown in you, for you are a woman and through woman the faith was preserved, and through woman it will be revealed: and you are this woman."

54.

On Tuesday in the chapel of Saint-Jacques she was enraptured and the voice told her: "You will be led to the interrogation but do not be afraid for you will have the heart of a lion. You are confirmed in divine knowledge and you will be given wings and transported into the desert."

55.

In the year of Our Lord 1386 she heard mass in the chapel of Saint-Jacques and several times before that the voice had told her to send a message to Lord Jean who was then archbishop of Toulouse to tell him

---

49. Pope Clement VII in fact limped in real life (see Valois, *La France et le Grand Schisme*, 1:81), but there are also symbolic aspects to this handicap. Saint Birgitta of Sweden, for example, saw Pope Gregory XI as a paralyzed man whose lack of willpower prevented him from returning to Rome (see Hans Aili, ed., *Revelationes. Book IV* [Stockholm: Almqvist and Wiksell, 1992], 394).

that these things [her revelations] concerned him. And she prayed to God to tell her what to say. And she was enraptured and the voice said: "Tell him that my words are already fulfilled when I said to my disciples: 'There will be signs in the sun, and the moon, and the earth' [Mt 24:29 and Lk 21:25]. Everything has been fulfilled. The sun signifies the true pope [of Rome]; the moon signifies the cardinals [of Avignon] who do not want to receive the sunlight, that is, the true pope. It is known that moonlight is dim and therefore they will remain dim and shadowy, just like the moon which does not receive the sunlight, but quickly the sun will pour out its light over the whole world. And the moon, that is, the true cardinals, will receive the sunlight. The stars are the doctors [of the Church] who must tell the truth but do not dare to do so. The earth stands for the great princes of this world who do not do justice. And you are my arrow that will pierce the hearts of the deceivers, and you will tell them that they will be measured by the same measure they use themselves."

She said: "Lord, if you measure them by the same measure they use, no one will be saved." The voice answered: "Do not be afraid for I am not like the other kings and princes who want vengeance, but I want them to convert. But I tell you that it would be easier to create a new world than to convert certain people." And she said: "Lord, did you not know that human nature is sinful?" And he answered: "Yes, but I gave them free will so that no one will have an excuse. And I tell you not to doubt these things, for heaven and earth will pass but the words that I tell you will not pass, and they will all be proven true. And just as the deluge came when no one expected it and Noah built the ark, the Son of Man will come when no one expects him [Mt 24:37-39]."

And later during high mass she had the same vision and was told: "You should know that they cannot deceive the Church Triumphant but only the Church Militant which will be in danger but will not perish." And this happened on the day of the conversion of Saint Paul [January 25].

56.

As it was written above in another chapter, her confessor had asked secretly for a sign from Our Lord to tell him whether he should write down the things she told him.[50] And he was given a sign and she revealed to him that he had a great illness in his heart. And he still did

50. See above, 2.2.

not want to write unless he were given another sign, for example, that God would take away his eyesight. And right away his eyesight became so bad that he could see only with his glasses on. And he still did not want to write, although many remarkable things happened to him in confirmation of the holy Catholic faith.

57.

In the same year on July 29, a Sunday, a priest was chanting the first mass and she complained to Our Lord: "Lord, how should I believe if my confessor doubts the things I say?" And she was enraptured and the voice told her: "Do not be afraid. Remember the things that I told and showed you. Just as I was abandoned at the time of my Passion so you will be abandoned, and just as my mother remained alone and disconsolate so you will remain alone and disconsolate. You will be abandoned by your confessor and every human creature, and my power will be manifest in your tribulations."

58.

On August 7 she was hearing mass from her confessor and prayed, weeping copiously, for the state of the Church, that it please God to take away this great error, the Schism,[51] and she was enraptured and the voice told her: "Send a message to the inquisitor, this deceiver of the faith who does not want to know the truth, that the words of Daniel have been fulfilled: 'When you see in a sacred place desolation and abomination, he who has ears will hear, for the day of misfortune and malediction is close; it is close for those who fornicated with the woman and have drunk the wine of indignity [see Dan 5:23 and 9:21–27]' And do not have any doubts, for it is written that no council can argue with me, who am the eternal God [see Mt 10], and all the things you will say will be a confirmation of the faith."

59.

The next day, which was a Wednesday, she heard mass in the chapel of Saint-Jean and prayed for the inquisitor; and she doubted the vision described above. She was enraptured and the voice told her: "Do not be afraid to send the letter, for they [the council of Toulouse] can be compared to Pilate's wife who wanted to prevent my Passion [Mt 27:19] so that the blessed would not receive their glory. And they are

---

51. The Catalan text reads *cisme d'error* indicating that the division of the Church was a grave error on the part of Christians.

just like that, those who do not want to know the truth nor want the truth to be made known."

60.

That same night before going to sleep she was in her oratory and prayed, weeping and crying, as described above. She was enraptured and the voice told her: "Send this request, as I have already told you."

61.

On Monday, August 13, at dawn after a night spent in prayer, she prayed to Our Lord weeping and crying more than she normally did. She was enraptured and it seemed to her that she was in a big church where there were many men and women, eight or six of them,[52] and there was a crucifix, and the crucified came down from the cross and became a man. She knelt down in order to adore him but she thought she was unworthy of touching him; and she wanted just to kiss his toenails but she did not dare, thinking herself unworthy. Then he took her by the hand and told her: "Do not be afraid." And then she kissed his hand and he said: "I will behave like a rich lord or a man who is furious." And she saw that he was beating these women with whips, and they fell down like dead in a heap. And he said to the men: "Put me back on the cross the way I was." And the men took the cross, put it on the ground, and put him back the way he had been. And she breathed deeply and marveled at the vision she did not understand. Then she went back to praying to God that he protect the Church.

62.

On the Day of Our Lady in August [August 15] after midnight, when she had said her prayers and prayed for the same purpose as mentioned above, she was enraptured and the voice told her: "The vision you saw the other day was true. The women you saw, whom I beat, are those people who fornicated and still fornicate with the woman and have drunk the wine of indignity. I was already once crucified and they crucified me again, and this is a greater offense than was the one Pilate committed when he delivered me to my death, for they did not want to adhere to the true pope I had created but created another one. And all the cardinals were there, but the true election was that of

---

52. The significance of these numbers is unclear.

the other one, that is, the first one.[53] And I will behave like a rich lord or a man who is furious."

And she said: "Lord, you will not behave as you say for you are always in your glory, and you will not act like a vengeful man. Rather, you will do good like the Lord full of mercy that you are. For your mercy is greater, Lord, than are their faults. Lord, I am the one who wants to bear their pains, provided they are not eternal." And the voice said: "The things I tell you, write them down and send them to the inquisitor, and he shall send them to the college [of cardinals] in Avignon. And if they believe you and want to correct themselves and repent of their iniquities I will forget [their faults], but if they do not want to believe you, I will do with them as it is said in the Scriptures: 'Out with you, cursed by my father from the beginning of the world, and there will be no more time, for you carry the sign of the malediction without end.'"[54] And these things were shown to her continuously, at least eight times, on the day following the feast of the Assumption. And around the hour of none she was told: "Send this message to the inquisitor."

63.

On the next to last day of August around noon she was praying in church. She was enraptured and saw the inquisitor and above him an angel who held a drawn and bloody sword above him. The voice said: "It would be better for the inquisitor to govern his own soul than those of others. I tell you that if he does not do the things I ask him to do through you and that I tell him about in my messages, an angel will come who will turn everything topsy-turvy, for the time has come for the Son of Man to show his power."

And she said: "Lord, you are not the Son of Man but the Son of God." And the voice responded: "By the woman is signified the man." She said: "Lord, give me some signs so that people will believe me, for I am too great a sinner for people to believe me." The voice answered: "I tell you that all this can only be accomplished through a miracle, and it is a great miracle that such a sinful woman as you should explain the Holy Scriptures to them, for you have never learned anything about them. And you have explained to them the Holy Trinity, the Holy Incarnation, and the Holy Sacrament of the

---

53. Of the sixteen cardinals that elected Urban VI in April 1378, thirteen were present at the election of Clement VII in September.

54. This passage echoes Matthew 25:41.

Altar, all the things that are hidden from the demon, and he would never dare or be able to confess them.[55]

Part 3

The things that follow were revealed to Lady Constance in Toulouse, and through her to her son. And they were transmitted in a letter to the confessor of the said lady when she was imprisoned.

1.

First, one day when she was praying to Our Lord the divine voice came to her and told her: "Do not be afraid, for it is time to gather the herd of my sheep and for the weak and sick sheep to be separated from the healthy ones. And I will tell them: 'Get away from here, you who are cursed by my Father, go to the eternal fire that has called you from the beginning of the world.'" And this was told to her many times.

2.

Another time two ships were shown her, and she was in one of them. The one in which she traveled experienced a moment of danger but got out of it quickly, but the other one entered into this peril and was destroyed. And Our Lord God told her that the ship she was in was the Holy Church of Rome, which can be in danger but cannot perish. And the other ship signified the antipope of Avignon and the College of anticardinals as well as all their followers, who, says Our Lord, are part of the Church of God but are infidels against the Church of God of Rome. They will perish just like the ship that signifies them, which perished and sank to the bottom.

3.

On Good Friday the voice of Our Lord told her: "The kings of this earth have their procurators that govern their people, and they are responsible for their government. Know that I am the eternal king, and

---

55. This passage evokes other cases of "unlearned" women teaching male clerics learned doctrine. A striking example is Angela of Foligno (d. 1309) who becomes a kind of theologian for the friar who records her life and visions. See Coakley, *Women, Men, and Spiritual Power*, ch. 6. Ursulina of Parma is of course another example. See par. 24a for the scene where she "teaches" the Trinity at the papal court in Avignon. The end of this paragraph is rather obscure; it seems to be an allusion to the demon's incapacity of understanding doctrine or the sacraments.

I have my procurators and governors who should govern their people for me, but they destroy it. Know also that they must account before me for the destruction they have wrought on my people whom I had created in my likeness."

4.

On another day the voice of Our Lord God offered her a similar parable: "A great king, when he wants to visit a place, sends ahead his message in letters sealed with his seal, and when the people of this region see the messenger and the sealed letters they prepare to receive their lord. You are my messenger and you carry my letters sealed with my seal, that is, the Holy Scriptures. You explain them and declare that they are my secrets and my seal. You told them that I would come soon and that they will be measured by the measure they themselves use, but there are few who prepare to receive me."

Part 4: Her Letters

What follows are the letters that Lady Constance transmitted to the inquisitor at God's command.

1. The first letter

Beloved and revered father, I commend myself humbly to your grace and I notify you that since I parted from you, I disregarded as much as I could the things that happened to me, but no matter how much I disregarded and fled them they still happened to me.[56] And my father [confessor] wanted to write nothing down except this letter. And may your wisdom know that many things were revealed to me, among them that I should write to you to remind you of the words that were said to Jonah, and many other things including threats.

Thus on a Wednesday, the day after the feast of Holy Mary, when high mass was being said, I was enraptured and the voice told me: "Write to the inquisitor that God notifies him that because he did not want to believe the things that I sent to him through you, I will inflict persecutions on the city of Toulouse. Tell him also that he is the caretaker of souls, and that this pertains to the faithful as well as to the infidels, and that the rebels will face malediction." Then I said: "Lord, they will not believe me." And the voice told me: "I command

---

56. Just as in the main text of the *Revelations*, Constance's visions and auditions are referred to as "these things."

you once, twice, three times to tell them, so that they will have no excuses. And you are not the one who is speaking, but it is the Holy Spirit that speaks in you."[57]

Therefore, my lord, you should convoke a council regarding these things. For, if this comes from God, I fear that God will avenge himself on you as well as on those who have meddled in this. And I believe that I have been exculpated, and if you can see your way to it please let my father [confessor] know that he should write down the things that happen to me, as he used to do. Also, you should know that I was afraid to send you this letter because of some things that my father said to me. But on the Saturday that was the last day of this month, during the elevation of the body of Jesus Christ, as I was praying fearfully and crying over these things, I was enraptured and told by the voice: "Do not be afraid to send this letter to the inquisitor, for it is time that the bad seeds should be thrown out from amidst the good ones, and that the viper full of poison and malice should lose its power."

Also, during high mass I saw an angel who was holding a drawn and bloody sword over the pope of Avignon as if he wanted to kill him.[58] May it please you to send me some response, for as much as I can I want to act according to your counsel.

2. Another letter

Reverend father, I notify you again of the things that are happening to me; they are even more numerous than before. But my confessor does not want to write them down. And you should know that much has been revealed to me, three times, so that I should write to you about it, but you took it badly. You should put your heart to guarding your sheep, since you are a pastor, for horrible days are approaching, and he who has ears will hear, and many other things [were revealed to me as well].

Also, on Quinquagesima Sunday[59] the voice told me: "Tell the inquisitor that before long he will be interrogated and that he should not fear death, and that the trial did not take place for nothing, and

57. At several points in his *vita* of Ursulina, Zanacchi notes that the Holy Spirit spoke through her.

58. See 2.63.

59. Quinquagesima (also known as Shrove Sunday) is the Sunday before Ash Wednesday, the day that signals the beginning of Lent, a period of fasting and contrition that ends on Easter Sunday.

that he should watch that the record corresponds to what was said at the trial, and that God tells him that he will have to render an account of the trial and the record."

3. Another letter

Reverend father, I am afraid that God will reprimand me for negligence if I do not hasten to write. And you should know that at mass yesterday, after the Scriptures had been read, the voice told me: "Write to the inquisitor that he should preach the misfortunes that are prepared for the evil ones, for the days of trembling are approaching. For this reason he should take care of the souls for it is his responsibility that, if the people of God is deceived out of ignorance, they will receive their punishment." And I answered: "My Lord God, they will not believe me." And the voice responded: "You will write that sometimes some king sends his messages to a certain place with his seal attached. And people believe the message even though the king comes from another kingdom. And you are not from another kingdom but from my own realm, and you carry my seal, that is, the Holy Scriptures, and for that reason the people should receive me well."

And he also said to me: "I tell you that I am not a demon, but the true God who has redeemed his people." And because I was still hesitating, he came back to me and said: "Why are you still doubting the things that I told you and commanded you to do? For the deadline is approaching and it is time that the things of which John spoke should be accomplished."

And another time, at eight in the morning when I was at table, the voice told me: "Convey to the inquisitor that which I proclaim loudly, namely that Antichrist's disciples are beginning to persecute the people of God throughout the world, and he who has ears will hear."

And another time he said: "Do not be afraid, for it has been ordained that I should reveal these things." Therefore, my lord, may it please you to convoke a council about all this, for there are many other things that I have not written to you. But considering what I have seen, you should have prayers said to God and arrange processions.

4. Another letter

Beloved lord, the more I resist the visions and revelations the more they continue, and even more so than before. Among other things, six months ago, I saw three cardinals in hell in great torment and pain, and there was one who was even more tormented than the others, and they said to me: "Cry out loudly to our brothers so that they will never have to suffer such torments." I rejected all this but often had this vision.

The evening before the feast day of Saint Cecilia it was revealed to me that the one who was thus tormented was Sir Pierre de la Barrière in his very own shape.[60] And I told my confessor, but he told me to reject this vision for he knew it was untrue. He knew of no one with the first name Pierre and said that this de la Barrière was a good person. Therefore he gave no credence to this revelation.

But I had the same vision another time and the voice told me: "You should know that what you have seen is true, no matter what your confessor says. Know that his first name is really Pierre and that he can be compared to a stone,[61] that is, the stone that brought the worst destruction to the path, and the stone on which the good seed fell but could not flourish [Mt 13:3-23]. He preached lies and false errors before the king. He is not content with his own damnation, but wants to pull others into damnation with him. He is called la Barrière because he established a barrier between me and himself." He showed me a great valley that had a high mountain on each side. He told me: "Just as these two mountains cannot approach each other, he can never approach me, and ask your father [confessor] how the person will be punished who offends the eternal God."

On the last day of January, as I said, I was enraptured during high mass, and throughout the mass and even after mass. And I was told that I should notify the inquisitor of these things, completely and at length and that my letter should be given to the collector[62] and the appellate judge.

Another time I saw him[63] all black like coal. Another time I saw how someone placed on his head a red hat that was all aflame; its roundness signifies the perfection of faith that cardinals should possess, and the color red signifies that they should die for the faith.[64]

---

60. For Pierre de la Barrière see note 22. Saint Cecilia's feast day is November 22.

61. The French word "pierre" means "stone."

62. The collector was a church official whose functions included the collection of moneys from the different congregations and their delivery to the ecclesiastical administration, as well as various other administrative duties.

63. Constance probably refers to Pierre de la Barrière here.

64. Different colors symbolize different kinds of martyrdom; red martyrdom is that of torment and death. But other interpretations of the color red also existed in the context of the

"And I am the true God of whom the Scriptures say that he sowed good seed. But Pierre de la Barrière has sown discord so much so that it has taken root. But the time has come for him to be torn out and thrown into hell. Know that the clamor of the people has been heard. And you, do not cease to clamor and do not hide the light of faith but exalt it as much as you can, so that the whole world will see it and no one can excuse himself."

My lord, I am afraid that through our failure to publish these things souls will be in great peril and the Christian faith will fall into disgrace. For when around the hour of prime a great star was seen, and after that many little stars that followed it, it was revealed to me that the greatest earthly man[65] prepared himself to pit all his power against Christianity and especially against the kingdom of France. Therefore, my lord, be diligent and do not prize your body and earthly honors more than the soul, for all of us must expose our bodies to death in order to save a single soul. And you should know that I am ready and prepared to die for God's honor and the salvation of the people.

And from now on I cannot refrain from crying out, for you should believe that these things have been revealed to me more than a hundred times, and I was always told to cry out for I owe more to God than to the world. And when I ask for a sign the voice tells me: "What other sign could you ask for than the one that says: 'Rise up for the Last Judgment.'" And therefore you must believe me, for I explain to you the Holy Scriptures when I do not know them. May the Holy Spirit protect you always, but answer me.

Written in Rabastens on February 14.

5.

She sent this letter to the inquisitor and to the collector and to Lord Yncart in the year 1384:

Dear lords, as you know, I have had many revelations and spiritual visions, and I still have them, and as many or even more than

---

Great Schism. Honoré Bovet, for example, in his *Tree of Battles* (1386-89), speaks of Pope Urban VI's cardinals' red hats saying: "what made [them] red? The blood of schism and sacrilege" (*L'Arbre des batailles*, ed. Ernest Nys [Brussels: Librarie Européenne, 1883], 27). On possible connections between Bovet and Constance see Blumenfeld-Kosinski, *Poets, Saints, and Visionaries*, 139.

65. This may be a reference to the emperor Wenceslas (reigned 1378–1400). Traditionally the emperor was opposed to the French king. In the Great Schism the emperor took the side of the Roman pope.

before. And you ordered me not to reveal them to anyone but my confessor and you. And I have written to you many times without getting any answer. My confessor does not want to write down anything and rejects [my visions], and so far I have obeyed him. But now I receive many revelations that concern the damnation or the salvation of the community. The kingdom of France is in great peril because of some grave treason and activities undertaken secretly under the pretext of peace; therefore, may it not displease you that I reveal them. For if they are true there will be great damnation, and you and I will be the cause of it, and it seems to me that I should not hide these things nor should anyone else. So please send me some secretaries to whom I can dictate the abovementioned revelations. For I have been ordered to tell them, to shout them and to trumpet them over the high mountains.[66]

Written on March 10.

6. Another letter

Father and lord, with humble recommendation I present myself to you. You should know that it has been revealed to me more than twenty times that a great prince of the realm of France has sent two important men to England under his seal, and that they have made league with the English on behalf of this prince. And they have sworn and denied God and his power and accepted the demon as their lord. And he[67] will give all his help and support to the English king against the young tree, that is, the French king, and if he can he will destroy the king and his realm, just as Pilate, when he was governor of Jerusalem, did not recognize our God who was from Jerusalem.

But after that a crane with a vermilion head[68] will come and destroy him, just as Vespasian destroyed Pilate. Then there will be a great alliance between the French king and the crane, and the king will be partly ruled by the crane. And soon the cow will be in the shadow of the flower, and it will put the rightful pope on his throne.[69]

---

66. Constance may refer here to the Biblical story of Joshua, who directed the Israelites to blow trumpets and shout to destroy the walls of Jericho (Jo 6); Constance may think of herself as Joshua leading a charge with priests and people against the enemy city and inhabitants of Avignon. See also Joel 2:1–2, announcing the coming doom with trumpet sounds.

67. It is not clear whether Constance means the prince or the demon here.

68. See above, 2.26.

69. The cow is part of the arms of the count of Foix-Béarn, Gaston Fébus; the flower probably stands for the fleur-de-lys of the French king.

Afterwards they will leave for the Holy Passage [crusade]. But in the meantime the king must watch out for Flanders, for I believe they[70] will be punished for the persecution that took place there. For it was neither just nor pleasing to God.[71]

May all these things be transmitted to you, for you know who is the prince in question. And I have been ordered to shout and trumpet the great betrayals. There are many other things to say but it would take too long to write them down.

Written on May 2. Thanks be to God.

Finito libro sit laus et Gloria Christo. Amen. Amen.

---

70. Constance may refer to the Flemish here.

71. For Flanders see the introduction.

Life of the Blessed Ursulina of Parma
by Simone Zanacchi

To the Reverend Mother in Christ Lady Magdalena Sanvitale, abbess of the Benedictine monastery of San Quintino in Parma, and to all the other nuns joyously serving their bridegroom Jesus Christ in that community, Brother Simone Zanacchi of Parma, useless servant of Christ and the unworthy prior of the Carthusian house of Saints Mary and Jerome at Montello near Treviso, offers shared hope for eternal life in the precious blood of the Immaculate Lamb.

1. There comes to mind, Reverend Mother, this declaration from the Holy Scriptures: "It is good to conceal a king's secret but honorable to reveal God's works."[1] Frequently reading over this idea on my heart's desk,[2] I am inflamed by the ardor of your outstanding faith. For you have deigned to choose and compel me, lacking in eloquence and poor in both expression and knowledge, to produce something out of the poverty of my understanding in fulfillment of your holy desire. Therefore, I do what you have often asked: relate with my clumsy pen the life and customs of the blessed Ursulina of Parma, whatever I might discover locally in writing or hear from trustworthy people.[3] I seek not to offer loveliness of language but instead to convey the truth about Ursulina's life for you and the other nuns who live there in the monastery where her holy body rests in peace.[4] As much as pious ardor calls me to satisfy fully your holy

---

1. The author quotes Tobit 12:7, from a speech in which the angel Raphael tells the virtuous Tobit and his son Tobias that they should proclaim the blessings God has granted them to reward their faithful merit. The reference anticipates three key themes of Ursulina's life: divine direction, saintly intervention, and recompense for good works.

2. The use of various parts of the body as metaphors for objects or ideas was even more frequent in the later Middle Ages than in our own times. The heart, in particular, can be almost anything, metaphorically.

3. Zanacchi, then, will rely on written documentation available in and around Parma plus oral tradition he considers reliable. He is likely to have had few if any firsthand accounts, since he wrote over sixty years after Ursulina's death. See also section 2 and section 7.

4. The writing of a saint's biography or *vita* ("life") was part of the process of having a person declared a saint by the papacy in the Middle Ages. Abbess Magdalena evidently wanted to have Ursulina, whose body was buried in her convent, declared a saint. To hold the relics of a recognized saint would increase the spiritual reputation and authority of the community. It could also bring material advantage in the form of pilgrims who, attracted to worship at the tomb of a holy person, often made contributions to the institution where it lay.

desire in this undertaking, to an equal degree the assorted labors, cares, and business arising from the office of prior with which I have been honored keep me from complying as I want. For the merits of my own life are not sufficient that I am confident in my ability to grasp worthily in mind and soul the deeds and life of so outstanding a virgin. It happens that on this subject men of faithful life and outstanding knowledge and eloquence have gathered up much material for this purpose from here and there, and following on the streams of their exuberant eloquence, I would for good reason be marked by presumptuousness if I tried to introduce a few more drops except that the faithfulness of your prayers—along with your pledge that my account (which I gathered together, with great difficulty, from numerous books in Latin and vernacular tongues), howsoever it emerges, will be accepted and you will consider it as a comfort for the people of this region—incites me to this labor.[5] But if by chance I offer anything here less carefully than I should, I pray that either you piously remove the offending matter or preserve it with the pardon of patience, seeking faith and love in my writing rather than charm.

2. Therefore, most beloved Mother in Christ, and you highly devout mothers, all together a singular exemplar of religion, inspired by your celestial prayers I will take up the task you command according to the power of my small talent. I make known, albeit in rustic style, to you, who know truth, the scattered material taken from others, seeing as they failed to set down things heard rather than experienced.[6] I am afraid and judge myself unworthy to sound forth the life and merits of so very renowned a virgin with insipid elegance and ignorant style amidst the literary refinement of learned people, whom I beg to want the account itself more than they ponder our uncultured discourse.

---

5. Zanacchi, while continuing to declare that only his patrons' confidence and prayer on his behalf overcomes his sense of unworthiness to write about Ursulina, makes two additional points. First, there is much material about Ursulina already written in florid Latin and other languages. (None of these is known to have survived, although there were still some left in the late eighteenth century: see Affò, *Vita della Beata Orsolina*, 10, n. 1). Secondly, Ursulina's story is meant to console and perhaps inspire Christians in and around Parma. The extreme grammatical complexity of this sentence, in ironic counterpoint to authorial protestations of ignorance and unworthiness, is typical of hagiography. *Captatio benevolentiae*, the "reaching for kindness" addressed to readers, was also a rhetorical feature of letterwriting and works on prayer and meditation. Zanacchi continues to beg pardon for his poor style in learned and convoluted sentences in the next section, where the translation divides them for ease of comprehension.

6. Again, the author alludes to oral tradition as a source of his account.

Let them, I say, seek out my pious thoughts rather than my pen's dullness.[7] I want them to know, too, that I, bound by your unceasing prayers, imposed on my shoulders a weight too great for them to bear. But the command was so forceful that I was unable to refuse what I did not want—and greatly feared. Moreover, although I know I am totally inadequate for and unworthy of such work owing to the paucity of my gifts, nevertheless I am equally compelled by great devotion to this same most famed virgin I know I have sustained for a long while. Putting aside fear and supported by great hope, I will make myself ready. Finally, encouraged by your prayers and the intercessions of the holy virgin Ursulina herself and protected in the highest degree by certain hope, I will fit my talent to this little work as much as I am able. If by chance I say too little or keep superfluously silent about whatever the greatness of this kindly virgin appears to demand, then please, good mothers, pardon my ignorance. I will have one concern above all: to touch on many things briefly, lest prolix detail incites boredom in readers and hearers.[8] Trusting in the grace of the Holy Spirit, I shall begin.

3. There was a most righteous man named Pietro, who walked in all goodness before God and men. He was a native of that golden city called Parma, outstanding among other Italian towns for both nobility and antiquity. Although out of zeal for chastity Pietro had shunned marriage after his first wedding and instead committed himself (insofar as he was able) to constant prayer to the Lord,[9] one day as he prayed to the Lord in deep concentration of heart and mind a command came from the heavens, saying, "Pietro, take Bertolina as your wife." When he had married his first wife, this Bertolina, who was afterward his second

---

7. The wise people from whom the author seeks pardon are female (*quas*): the compliment is to the nuns of San Quintino and other female readers.

8. Zanacchi stresses that he anticipates a wide and mixed audience for his portrait of Ursulina, one that might learn of her life by means of his account, but not necessarily through *reading* it. That is, he imagines all or part of his text might be read, after translation into everyday dialect, to the illiterate or those who cannot read Latin.

9. The phrase *ut poterat*, "insofar as he was able," suggests that the widowed Pietro was obliged to work for a living in one of the many occupations associated with late-medieval urban life. The father-to-be of Ursulina was not of extraordinary wealth or birth, or else the author, in keeping with traditions of hagiography, would say so. At the same time, Ursulina's travels suggest some measure of familial financial resources. Pietro, then, was likely of the prosperous artisanal or merchant classes, as also suggested by the end of this section, where he obtains reassurance about Bertolina's lineage before marrying her.

wife, was in her mother's womb.[10] Pietro, stunned by the utterance and quite frightened, too, began to ponder anxiously concerning a command of this sort granted to him. More than a little uncertain and not knowing where to turn, especially since he had hitherto rejected such a marriage, finally he made up his mind and decided to obey divine will.[11] After painstaking and lengthy investigation, he found the said Bertolina, formerly unknown to him, and when he recognized her virtues and ancestry, he took her in marriage.

4. Bertolina, after many years of marriage and several daughters, was home alone one notable day, thinking with deep concentration about the vanities of this world, the briefness of human life, and also about heavenly glory and the happiness of blessed spirits. In a trance, meditating a long while on the uniqueness, sublimity, and greatness of the Trinity and compelled by the sweetness of her meditation, she burst forth in great cries, for the Holy Spirit had chosen her. That night, the same Holy Spirit informed Bertolina's husband Pietro in dreams that the most precious fruit of their marriage was to come forth from her. Two weeks later, it was revealed to Pietro as he slept that the bishop of the city told him he should stay with him. Pietro refused to do so out of consideration for his household and wife. Nevertheless, the bishop exhorted Pietro to do as he asked without misgivings. Pietro gave this reply: "I will go home and consult with my wife." Having given his promise to make a response to the bishop's plea, Pietro hastened home, and behold, he heard an angel calling him. When he told the curious angel about the bishop's request and that the bishop had accepted a respite of a month for Pietro's decision, the angel said to Pietro, "Satisfy the bishop with a reply in one year and a month." When that deadline had been agreed to by the bishop, the angel said to Pietro, "Your wife is pregnant now and will bear a daughter who will be greatly pleasing to God." "How do you know these things?" asked Pietro. "I am an angel, assigned to watch over you. Know that for five years your daughter will be incapable of any steady step, amidst great mystery, since the Lord will reveal

10. In late-medieval Italy, men tended to postpone first marriage, while women often married before age twenty: see David Herlihy, *Medieval Households* (Cambridge: Harvard University Press, 1985), 103–11, passim. Pietro was likely well into middle age if he had been widowed for a considerable period before marrying Bertolina. She, on the other hand, may have been in her teens.

11. Zanacchi stresses Pietro's reluctance to remarry with the verb *abiecere*, with its overtones of debasement, abandonment, and defeat.

many things to her. But in her sixth year, she will begin to walk; in her fifteenth year she will begin to talk and in her sixteenth she will walk perfectly and speak perfectly what the Lord will reveal to her." With these words, the angel vanished.[12] Awakened from his dream, Pietro thought intently about its meaning and indeed told Bertolina about it and other things afterward in their turn. Pietro lived a year and eight months after this dream-vision.[13]

　　　　5. In due course the blessed Ursulina was born of Bertolina, on the morning of May 14, 1375. Because of her mother's weakness, the blessed Ursulina had to feed at others' breasts, which she did willingly, except that she not only refused to suckle but even shrunk from the touch of a woman thought to be an adulteress.[14] That was a wonder, but more marvelous still was it that the other nurses who saw this were stunned and said, "Truly, if this little girl lives, she will be something great, for she already foretells things to come." Listen, I pray you, to what followed. In her fourth month, when she had not known how to speak before and would not again for many months afterward, Ursulina burst forth in a strong voice with these words: "O God, God my Father!" Hearing this, her mother was quite surprised and kept the utterance a secret in her heart's treasury. The baby girl had a sister, age four, who often saw two men standing by the blessed Ursulina's cradle, one each on the right and the left, dressed in extremely bright robes. The girls' mother tried to see if this was actually true by several tests. Rebuking her daughter, she said, "Are you asleep [when you see them]?" "No, I'm not sleeping," came the reply, "but when they go over to her, I lift up my head completely and I watch them in bright light—it's true what I say." Bertolina fell silent. Much later, she asked Ursulina about the two men. Ursulina said, "One of them was the blessed apostle Peter, whom God appointed as my teacher. The other never wanted to reveal his identity." But it can be believed in good faith that it was St. Paul or an angel sent by him. For just as in this

12. The hagiographer has shot this paragraph through with biblical echoes, the most evident being the conception of Isaac in the old age of his parents, Abraham and Sarah (Gn 17 and 21) and the Annunciation to Mary of the miraculous birth to come (Lk 1). It also recalls the story of Tobit, from whose story Zanacchi extracted a sort of epigraph for his *vita* in section 1: just as Ursulina will recover from her disabilities, Tobit is cured of blindness and experiences general good fortune in his old age.

13. See section 8, below, for an explanation of Pietro's vision.

14. This first miracle aside, Zanacchi's description offers another hint at the social and economic status of Ursulina's parents: they were members of an urban middle class in which wet-nursing was a common practice.

mortal life the two were companions, so Paul would not be parted from Peter after death.[15]

6. At age four, the blessed Ursulina was not yet able to walk steadily, just as the angel had warned her father.[16] Her mother, in church one day and seized by divine inspiration, offered Ursulina to God on the altar of the blessed Peter Martyr, in the chapel of the Dominican friars.[17] As soon as she touched that altar, Ursulina gained as sure and steady a step as her age would allow. One day, while she was a girl of six, she wandered here and there on the road near her house and lo, two men of venerable appearance, unknown to bystanders, moved close to the blessed virgin Ursulina and placed their hands on her head, saying, "This girl was chosen by God and reserved for a great miracle." From that time, the blessed virgin began to have marvelous visions. The first was on the first day of the year and concerned the end of the world and the resurrection of the dead.[18] Ursulina also began to know God through her human understanding, all of which she experienced on her own and in silence. She was a stranger to all worldly desires, devoting herself mind and spirit and in all reverence to the Lord. Seeing this, her mother's neighbors said, "Truly your daughter is too proud and restrained. She never takes part in our conversation like other people." When her mother passed this along, Ursulina replied, "For what reason should I abandon the company of my Lord Jesus Christ and the saints on account of those women? Thus the Lord has called me, and I serve and follow Him."

7. When Ursulina reached her ninth year, remaining humble as time and place demanded, she began, by the action of grace, to make others sharers in her visions and revelations from God. She knew this meant she would give praise in all things and glory to God

---

15. Ursulina's two guardians, then, were St. Peter, the first bishop of Rome, that is, the first pope, appropriate for someone with Ursulina's destiny, and St. Paul, the great exponent of the budding cult of Christianity in the first century, who like Ursulina traveled extensively.

16. Reference to what we now call developmental delay, along with the adult Ursulina's tiny stature, suggest some childhood illness or disability, as foretold by the angel who visited her father. In any case, Ursulina was evidently an odd little girl.

17. St. Peter Martyr, a Dominican preacher and inquisitor, was assassinated in 1252 by heretics. His altar is a fitting place for the reception of Ursulina into God's service, since he was a fellow Italian and enemy of heterodoxy.

18. Perhaps because Ursulina is such an unusual figure, her biographer takes pains to make her first vision utterly in keeping with orthodox Christian teaching, just as her celestial guardians in infancy were founders of the Church. Orthodoxy is equally stressed in the next section.

and that consequently the power and great goodness of God would be celebrated and benefit accrue equally to her neighbors and others. However, she always presented herself humbly when telling people about her visions, saying, for instance, "A person saw this vision; determine what it is" or "I heard from someone, try to discern if it came from the Father, the Son, the Holy Spirit, or an angel or saint."[19] Thenceforth God himself and our Lord Jesus Christ deemed it worthy to reveal many, many secrets and divine mysteries in succession as long as Ursulina lived, as the many volumes written about these revelations bear witness. I avow that I have seen and read them all with due reverence.[20] But so great was the blessed virgin Ursulina's humility and gentleness that she tried to make known what God had revealed to her with all restraint and as time and place demanded.

8. Knowing the divine will concerning what she was to do, Ursulina refused to listen to preachers' sacred public utterances. "I do not refuse," she told her mother, "because I scorn the holy lessons of preachers, but because instead I obey the commands of Him whom they preach. Since God himself, the Lord Creator of all things, has decided to reveal things to the human race through me, He forbids me to go hear public preaching until whatever He has decided to reveal to me is written down, lest those men might by chance think that I learned from their sermons what God himself wanted to reveal through me." Therefore she never wanted to put on any monastic habit, only spiritual clothing as devout and humble as she could bear. When this blessed virgin was in her fifteenth year, she had the following vision. It appeared to her as if she was in her heavenly homeland, in the presence of our Lord Jesus Christ, and that the Lord himself said to the blessed virgin's father, standing there alongside Him, "Is this not your daughter?" Pietro replied, "You know, Lord." And the Lord Jesus Christ spoke to him again. "Is this not your daughter?" Her father answered, "She is your daughter, Lord." And He asked a third time, "Is this not your daughter?" and when he replied, "Lord, she is," the Lord said, "Now tell your daughter about the vision you had about her when she was still in her mother's womb." Pietro did as he was

---

19. Here and periodically through the next several sections, Zanacchi emphasizes that from childhood, Ursulina subjected her revelations to public scrutiny, allowing evaluation of the kind discussed at the beginning of the account of Constance of Rabastens' revelations. The sources of the visions are all, like the subject matter mentioned previously and subsequently, completely orthodox.

20. None of this material has survived.

told. Then the Lord said to him, "It was I, that bishop to whom you promised you would return, wanting to remain with me with your wife's permission."[21] When all this had passed, the vision faded away.

9. The Lord himself clearly showed the blessed Ursulina visions nearly every day and disclosed very profound revelations. Then He ordered that she have written down everything He had revealed to her.[22] When she was wondering to whom this duty should be entrusted, she asked, "Whom should I choose, Lord?" The Lord told her that a certain old man, a priest of proven virtue, was suitable for this task. After this old man had flatly refused three times, in the end, knowing the will of God, he did not hesitate to take on the task. At intervals over the next three years, the priest set down several volumes of writing at the blessed Ursulina's dictation. Besides him, Ursulina had at various times and places six other transcribers of her revelations. The first was Lord Tommaso Fosio, from Parma, the aforementioned priest; the second was Master Niccolò of the order of hermits; the third Lord Anthony of Milan, an official of the antipope Clement in Avignon; the fourth Lord Jacopo Sibinago, the official in charge of legal cases in the Roman curia; the fifth Master Amico, a physician in the Roman curia; the sixth the great armor-bearer and commander Gherardo Aldighieri, from Parma; and finally, the outstanding learned man Lord Donnino Garimberti, from Parma.[23]

21. See above, section 4; Pietro had been dead for many years at the time of this vision. The arithmetic is confusing, however. Perhaps the thirteen months mentioned above were to start at Ursulina's birth, giving Pietro twenty months to live when the angel told him about his blessed daughter in the womb, or perhaps after thirteen months, Pietro agreed to join the bishop, that is to die in Christ, in another several months.

22. It is not clear that Ursulina herself could write or even read; she seems to have gained all her knowledge through revelation.

23. Ursulina's scribes are a diverse lot reflecting her unusual career: clerics, learned men, and at least one layman, who worked in Parma, Avignon, and Rome. The priest Tommaso was of noble local family (Affò, *Vita della Beata Orsolina*, 6, n. 1). Niccolò was likely a leader of Parma's house of the Order of Hermits of St. Augustine, formed in 1244, when Pope Innocent IV united several groups of hermits and imposed on them the Rule of St. Augustine, a short outline of communal religious life written around 400 CE by the great North African bishop and theologian Augustine of Hippo (354–430). On Anthony of Milan, see below, section 27. Jacopo and Amico are officials in the service of a Roman pope, probably Boniface IX, whom Ursulina met on two different occasions. Apparently both a lawyer and a doctor examined this young woman amidst her visions, a fact Zanacchi does not mention otherwise but in keeping with the interest in discernment of spirits in this *vita* (and in the *Revelations* of Constance of Rabastens). On Gherardo Aldighieri, see the Introduction. Donnino is the second local scribe, the third if Niccolò was indeed from Parma. The order

10. This esteemed virgin was very small but adorned with a venerable face; because of her calm ways, she was beloved and welcomed by all. She had remarkable knowledge of Holy Scripture, that is, concerning the Trinity, the Incarnation of God, His birth, angels, and heavenly glory. Many marveled at her wisdom and declared that the elegance of her discourse exceeded all womanly ability, for everybody took away from her an extremely clear solution to any difficulty. Even more amazing, a unique gift of God, is that although she spoke so sublimely, elegantly, and profoundly about all these matters, nobody could ever perceive any hint of boasting on her part. She put everything forth with humility, with a certain inner and outer gentleness, and with such charm of language that listeners judged that within a human body she spoke beyond the body, without any human effort. Fasting, self-denial, prayers, and other praiseworthy works that she busied herself in performing equally for the love of God as for the fear of hell: all these she labored to do with all care and prudence, away from the gaze of others. In all of her works, both spiritual and bodily, she observed discretion, for she knew it is the mother of all virtues.[24] She went often to confession, and every month received the Body of Christ, as secretly as she was able, so as not to be considered excessively spiritual by others.[25] Every day and every hour she feasted within herself on spiritual nourishment from the Lord.

11. God deemed it worthy to show the following vision to the blessed virgin before she started on a certain journey. In accustomed fashion, she drew His spirit like a sword from its sheath and understood through the vision how much strength, wisdom, and love He imparted to her. It seemed to her that she was led into a great church, where she saw the Lord walking about, looking all around. When the blessed virgin Ursulina asked Him what He sought, He replied, "I am looking for a seat on which I might rest, but I cannot

---

of the list is probably not chronological, since it is likely that Jacopo and Amico heard Ursulina during her first visit to Rome, which was before the dictation to Anthony of Milan in Avignon; perhaps the visions Zanacchi read were preserved in this order.

24. That discretion is the mother of virtues is a medieval commonplace.

25. Frequency of communion and the nature of Eucharistic devotion and experience were a topic of intense and often gender-inflected debate in the later Middle Ages: see Caroline Walker Bynum, *Holy Feast and Holy Fast: The Religious Significance of Food to Medieval Women* (Berkeley: University of California Press, 1987), 57–60. Perhaps Ursulina, aware of the intense Eucharistic mysticism of Catherine of Siena and concerned that she not be considered a conscious imitator of a famous holy woman, was at pains to keep different devotional habits.

find one anywhere." She sat down on the ground and said to Him, "Lord, sit here now, and rest on my knees." He did so. After a short while, He rose and led the blessed Ursulina into a house where, as it seemed to her, He drew an oversized cup of fine wine from a cask and then told her to take a little. When she had tasted and drunk, she remarked to herself, "There are some people who, when they are drunk, are unable to speak, but after tasting this pure wine, I see further and understand more clearly than usual." Then the blessed Ursulina woke up and finding herself far more inspired than before, gave great thanks to God, for through the vision she understood a great present and future mystery, as will become evident below.

12. Once when she was receiving the most blessed body of Christ on Easter and rejoiced inwardly with spiritual gladness, the voice of the Lord came to her, saying, "Now prepare yourself to go where I send you."[26] Ursulina did as she was told at once. When her mother had been informed of these instructions, she sighed, saddened, and said, "Alas! I am old and full of days and you are so young: how can we go forth without a guide?" Ursulina said to her, "Mother, have no doubts. Shall we worry when the Lord is with us, and shall we be without a companion? Heaven forbid! Let us only obey the Lord's commands, and He will be our helper and protector in all things." When all were ready to depart—the blessed virgin along with her mother, a cousin, and another honorable woman—Ursulina said, "Lord, where do you want me to go?" The Lord replied, "Go to the city of Avignon in France, where the pseudo-pope Clement lives. Don't you know that there is a great schism in Christendom because of him? Head that way."

13. Hastening on the journey according to God's command, she decided to visit the church of the blessed Mary Magdalene in Provence.[27]

---

26. This was probably in 1393.

27. It is over 400 miles from Parma to Avignon, a long trip but not a difficult itinerary. Ursulina could have traveled along main routes, the durable Roman roads built many centuries earlier. The likeliest route would have taken the party first to Genoa, next westward along the Mediterranean coastline, moving inland toward Arles, and finally northward to Avignon—a journey of several weeks on foot, although in section 14 it is suggested that the heavenly guide showed Ursulina and her mother some shortcuts. Visiting the shrine of Mary Magdalene did not mean a great detour from the standard itinerary, for it was just off the main road, about 70 miles east of Arles. Mary Magdalene was the first of Jesus' disciples to whom he spoke after the Resurrection. According to legend, she spent her later years in Roman Gaul, now France. In the thirteenth century, a cave thought to be the Magdalene's home and bones in an early Christian sarcophagus were discovered near each other in central Provence. Pilgrimage to these two sites grew; Charles of Anjou (1227–1285), younger brother of

As the three[28] went along together, they were told that it was doubtful they could keep going without trouble from highway bandits. Hearing this, Bertolina was grieved and said to Ursulina, "Woe is us, daughter!" She replied, "Mother, have no doubt that the Lord will provide for us, just as He said through the prophet: 'Have no fear at their appearance, for I am with you and I will rescue you, says the Lord. For you will go where I send you and whatever I command you to say you will tell them. Fear not, says the Lord' [see Jer 1:8, 7]." While the blessed Ursulina and her mother looked for divine aid to enable them to go anywhere safely, a pilgrim overtook them unexpectedly. When they asked him where he was going, he answered that he was on his way toward the church of St. Mary Magdalene but not going all the way there. Ursulina looked carefully at his face and appearance, which were not those of a man but of an angel. She said to her mother, "Here is our guide, a sure companion for our journey. Let us confidently stick close to this traveler, whom the most benevolent Father Himself, the kindly hearer of our prayers, has placed in our sight."

14. Asked to be their companion, the pilgrim pretended that he did not want to stay with them, saying that he had never gone that way and even that he did not have such a long journey. Thus he seemed to be very uncertain. The blessed Ursulina said to him, "Why should we be in doubt? The grace of God and our Lord Jesus Christ will be with us, like a safe escort." This pilgrim (or rather messenger of God), with his angelic charm and downturned eyes and bowed head that showed who he really was, began the journey. The blessed Ursulina and her mother followed him. And so nearly every day this divine companion was with them, showing secret itineraries. He went along everywhere with equal steps, staying a stone's throw ahead of them so that he might be thought separate from those whose comrade and leader he was. When the blessed Ursulina and her mother were tired and went to rest in the shade of a tree, soon he, too, sat down in the shade of the next tree not far off. When they got back up, he quickly rose and prepared himself to proceed. He did not want to stay in the

---

the saintly King Louis IX of France, sponsored the construction of a large Gothic church to house the relics. Mary Magdalene became a great patron saint of the Order of Preachers, or Dominicans; it was in the Dominican church in Parma that Bertolina had offered the child Ursulina to God's service. The Magdalene, as a reformed sinner, was a favorite saint of pious laywomen, another way in which Ursulina's behavior is suited to her status.

28. The narrative is confused about the size of the party, said at the start to have been four. Here there are only three and only Ursulina and her mother are mentioned hereafter.

same lodgings with them, lest, as is believed, the reputation of the holy virgin be stained with some scandal.[29] Yet every morning they saw him going along ahead of them, and every day he offered them provisions for the journey. Although they had passed many days on the road, they never met a bandit, an enemy, or any other wicked man, even though the places through which they traveled were troubled on all sides with many conflicts of all sorts.[30] This was the Lord's doing; it is hardly marvelous that one traveling in accord with divine command is watched over by a celestial guardian.

15. When they had reached the place he had said he was going, since the journey had been completely safe for them all, he said to the blessed Ursulina and her mother, "I'm headed the other way now. That's your road ahead. Go on, free of doubt, and the peace of the Lord will be with you." The blessed Ursulina said to him, "I beseech you, through Him who redeemed us with his precious blood, that you not abandon us, since without you we will have no idea of the route." At last, showing himself defeated by their prayers, he acquiesced to the wish of the blessed Ursulina and her mother and as before he went along with them to St. Mary Magdalene as their scout and guide. When they had all visited the church of Mary Magdalene, the holy pilgrim said to them, "Now I have fulfilled your prayers and I go no further with you." Showing them a path, he said, "Go that way as far as the mountain you see not far off and in the valley you find there, ask directions from the natives who are tilling the soil and they will point you the right way." With these words, he departed and soon vanished from their sight. Bertolina, who had all along thought the pilgrim a man, was frightened by his sudden disappearance and said to the blessed Ursulina, "Tell me, daughter, who that was, our fellow-traveler for so many days who vanished so quickly from our sight?" The blessed Ursulina replied, "That was the blessed John the Evangelist, whom God gave us as a guide up until now."[31] Hearing this, Bertolina was filled with great joy. Going forth as they had been told, they found the laborers as the blessed John the Evangelist had predicted. When they

29. Dangerous as it might be for women to travel alone, it would be scandalous for them to travel with a male stranger they picked up along the way.

30. The later Middle Ages featured nearly constant political and military disturbances in northern Italy and France, and as Zanacchi suggests, even travelers on the holy business of pilgrimage were not immune from banditry.

31. Before his death, Jesus commended his mother Mary to the apostle John's care, so it is quite appropriate that it is John whom God sends to guard and guide these women.

had shown the women the right road, they let them pass, and the party at last arrived safely at the destination: Avignon.

16. Upon arrival, the blessed virgin Ursulina was afire with spiritual joy. Hands lifted toward heaven, she prayed to the Lord. "Lord Jesus Christ, greatest master and true light, since now I have arrived here safe and sound with your guidance in order to fulfill your command, pour forth your grace on me from above and fill my mouth with your eloquence. In that way I, the least of your handmaids and utterly unworthy, will be able to say whatever is pleasing to Your Majesty, since alone, Lord, I am profoundly ignorant." When she had made this sort of prayer, the Lord spoke to her. "Ursulina, fear not and believe, for I am with you wherever you wander. Go to this antipope and tell him whatever I inspire you to say." Thus by God's command the blessed Ursulina got access to the antipope through the pseudo-cardinal Peter of Puy.[32] Peter said to her, "What greeting and sign of respect will you make when you are brought in to him?" She replied, "Whatever the Holy Spirit inspires in my heart." When she was placed in the sight of the antipope himself, she genuflected, and with hands raised and eyes fixed on heaven, said in a loud voice, "Glory to the Father, and the Son, and the Holy Spirit." All assembled were astounded when they heard this greeting.[33]

17. The antipope commanded everyone to withdraw for a little while and ordered her to come closer to him. Ursulina conversed with him unceasingly for nearly an hour and a half with calm tongue, brave expression, and fearless mind. She concluded with these words, "You will learn that if you hesitate to carry out these things that I have laid out for you on behalf of our Lord Jesus Christ, your place in hell will be considered the equal of Lucifer's." The antipope was quite frightened at these words. Fearing others around would hear, he declared that he would grant her another audience on a day he would name, so to be able, at a chosen time, to prevent covert eavesdropping more easily. Rising from his throne, the antipope went with Ursulina

32. Peter Gerald was a devoted agent of Clement VII, a court clerk who advocated for the Avignon papacy on several diplomatic missions—an appropriate counterpart to Ursulina. For his loyalty, Peter Gerald was made bishop of Puy, in southern France, in 1384 and a cardinal in 1390. See Valois, *La France et le Grand Schisme*, 2: 439–40.

33. The *Gloria Patri* is an ancient expression of praise used extensively in medieval liturgies. Perhaps onlookers are surprised to hear a teenage girl using a phrase more often heard on the lips of priests instead of a direct greeting or compliment to the antipope. The whole scene described would have taken place in a large chamber of the papal palace among a considerable crowd of powerful men.

as far as the second door of his hall. When he assured the blessed Ursulina that he would do whatever he could on her account, she said loudly to him, "I would rather make a meal of tree bark than suffer to accept anything from you." With these words she departed. All the pseudo-cardinals were angry at the antipope because he had risen up from his throne for some girl and paid her such honor. He replied that he had not done so for the girl but the Lord who sent her.

18. On the appointed day, the blessed Ursulina went to the antipope. When he learned that she had come to see him, he was overtaken with such fear and trembling that he did not dare have her brought in and subject himself to her gaze. He was forced to send her back home unseen. The next day he ordered her to be summoned. Upon learning that she was just outside, a powerful terror took him, and his blood ran even colder than before. Again Ursulina was dismissed and told to return the next day. She was led to the antipope a third time. When her arrival was announced, he was overpowered by fright and shaken with fear even more fiercely than the first two times. Unfortunate man! In light of so many great signs, he should have received and listened to the blessed virgin with great reverence. Instead, driven by the power of the devil that he served instead of God, he sent her away like someone with plague.[34] Nor would he allow himself to endure the presence of someone he had previously revered with great honor. O wretch, most unhappy of men, wicked scorner of divine command and his own soul's salvation! Although much affected, alerted by Ursulina's profound knowledge, and forewarned of divine punishment, he put off recognizing his own great treachery and faithlessness toward both himself and his Church. The blessed Ursulina saw how pathetic the antipope was and how he was so in thrall to the great fear and trembling the devil had imposed that he did not dare admit her to his presence. Since he refused to learn God's will through her mouth, she said to a great crowd of listeners in Avignon, "I call forth and bear witness to heaven, earth, the sea, and everything in their embrace that I came to him to announce God's will, just as God Himself deemed worthy to order and command me to do." Having said this, she turned on her heel and leaving the city, returned to Parma without delay.

---

34. *Pestiferum* here has literal as well as figurative meaning. Although the most devastating episode of the Black Plague took place in the years 1347–50, when some areas of Europe lost half their population, the disease recurred less virulently every generation or so long afterwards. Furthermore, Avignon had been one of the first major European cities hit in 1347.

19. A few days passed. The blessed Ursulina was still very tired from her long journey and had not yet recovered her former strength when the Lord ordered her to go to Boniface, the supreme pontiff and true pastor of all the Lord's flock residing in Rome, and tell him everything that had happened with the pseudo-pope. As soon as she received the divine command, she moved her little body despite exhaustion. Putting all faith in her Lord Jesus, Ursulina hastened to Rome with quick step, unclouded mind, and eager devotion.[35] For she understood beyond all doubt that divine commandment must be carried out in word and in deed, with all bodily power, by every person. When she reached Rome, accompanied by her mother, ready opportunity bestowed by divine grace presented itself: after only a short delay, Ursulina entered into the sight of the supreme pontiff and described in detail everything as it had happened. Since Pope Boniface was reluctant to believe Ursulina's account, omnipotent God himself— the master and governor of all things heavenly, earthly, and infernal, who knows the future and arranges everything in time and space according to his ineffable order—made wondrous provision. A certain venerable Carthusian monk, a man most worthy for his faith and reverence, was present in Rome. He, too, had been at Avignon when the blessed Ursulina was engaged in the aforementioned business with the pseudo-pope. The monk had thus learned about everything, partly as an eyewitness, partly from trustworthy report. He made the doubting mind of the supreme pontiff more certain—as is quite evident in certain of his letters mentioning the matter that I have read myself.[36]

20. So thereafter the blessed Ursulina was received by the supreme pontiff and the cardinals of Holy Church and treated with due honor. What she said among them was taken on faith, undoubted, for truly they were in no doubt that she was a messenger of divine will. Therefore Pope Boniface, once Ursulina's deeds had been told and discussed in public consistory, together with the most reverend cardinals decided at last by the workings of divine wisdom to send ambassadors to the aforementioned antipope in the hopes of re-establishing the sacrosanct orthodox Church according to the blessed

---

35. It is about 300 miles from Parma to Rome via the old routes southward to central Italy from Ursulina's Po Valley home.

36. Here again, the author refers to materials no longer known to exist. Zanacchi himself was the head of a Carthusian monastery, as he notes at the beginning of his account of Ursulina.

virgin Ursulina's resolve.[37] For it was the blessed Ursulina's will that these representatives try with all their might to persuade the antipope and his pseudo-cardinals to refrain from resisting the Holy Apostolic See—and also warn the men in Avignon to beware of divine retribution. Like faithful Catholics, they should humble themselves in the assurance that great clemency, both divine and papal, would follow. Finally, the ambassadors were to remind those men that they did not want to be a threat or cause of damnation for themselves and others. Since the plan for a message of this sort pleased the supreme pontiff and all the cardinals, as if with one breath they promptly decided that they would choose no ambassadors to the forenamed antipope except the blessed Ursulina. For they realized from what had already happened that she was guarded by divine protection. Burning with the longing to save souls and bubbling over with the desire to carry out divine commandments, the blessed Ursulina, albeit a frail woman weakened from her earlier trip, was unafraid of a long journey and with cheerful heart offered, out of faith in God and for the purpose of making peace for the holy Mother Church, to return to the antipope and carry out the supreme pontiff's orders to the best of her ability. This pleased the pope wonderfully, and together he and the cardinals accepted the blessed Ursulina's vow.

21. Having received the apostolic benediction, the blessed Ursulina, along with her mother, returned to the antipope.[38] After great trouble and much delay, she reached Avignon, carrying a papal letter. Knowing that first she should seek out the house of God, she proceeded to visit the church of Saint-Didier in that same city.[39] There she met the pseudo-cardinal Peter of Puy, whom we have often mentioned already.[40] When he recognized her, he called her to his side and said, "Ursulina, where are you going? And where did you come from just now?" She replied, "The Love that bears all, carries all, and sustains all led me here again to you." When he inquired more

---

37. A consistory is an assembly of cardinals presided over by the pope. "Public" here means not that anyone could come but that some other invited participants, like Ursulina, were also present.

38. This trip was about 600 miles, assuming Ursulina traveled by land. She arrived in Avignon in early 1394.

39. There had long been a church in Avignon dedicated to St. Didier, but the Gothic building Ursulina entered was relatively new, built in the 1350s and decorated with murals dating to the time she worshiped there at the end of the fourteenth century.

40. See above, section 16.

specifically about the reason for her journey, she said, "The state of your souls torments me and turns me into a pilgrim and a foreigner." "What do you seek?" Peter asked. "I want, I hope for, I desire with my whole heart the salvation of your souls," she replied. Smiling, Peter responded, "You do seem, as you say, to hope for our souls' salvation very ardently and devotedly and with a thirsty soul. But if a ready opportunity presented itself, the pope and his cardinals would choose to kill you. Don't you know that they are currently concocting all manner of charges against you? Has it escaped your notice that each of them ponders how they might destroy you? Go back where you came from as quickly as possible; don't show your face in Avignon. And don't put off for a moment what I advise. Already I perceive your ruin being plotted should you delay your departure." But the blessed Ursulina, to whom the Holy Spirit gave eloquence and for whom love provided daring, was in no way frightened by these words. She said to Peter, "I beseech you now, if I have any powers of persuasion, I entreat, I plead, and I pray you: if it is possible, let it be reported without delay to your pope and all his cardinals that I have come to them again. I bear a message for them from the supreme pontiff and true vicar of our Lord Jesus Christ." But she did not show the letter at that time, holding it back for the moment.

22. Once the pseudo-pope and his cardinals had learned about the arrival of the blessed virgin, Clement ordered her to be summoned to him. Girding herself with a token of the glorious Cross and placing all her hope in the Lord Jesus Christ, in particular that she might effect the reunion of the Holy Church, she brought herself into the sight of the assembled men without the slightest hesitation, fearless. No gaze of men can have such power that it is able to frighten one armed with the Holy Spirit. Therefore, once in their presence, unfazed by the attention of such mighty men she began speaking with such steadfast expression and brave and ringing voice that she might have been thought to offer divine rather than human discourse. Since she spoke to them with unfurrowed brow, not one of them dared to return a menacing word—even though they had decided beforehand that Ursulina would end her life in agony. Oh, mightiest power of the divine Word and infallible arrangement of its wisdom in all things! This oration by a holy virgin—or rather by the Holy Spirit—lit up the minds of those men for whom the erection of the most wicked throne and prideful disdain had for a long time darkened the way of truth and the path of true understanding. Once they had heard

her, their reason was restored and the antipope and pseudo-cardinals approved of what she said. So the blessed virgin, granted permission by all to speak more fully, discoursed at greater length. She showed them, in a reasoned manner impossible to contradict, that it was not fitting for them to stand in opposition to the holy, orthodox Roman Church. Instead, they should all submit themselves to its correction with bowed heads.

23. The antipope, utterly defeated by such divine reasoning, decided to place his neck in the yoke of the sacred Roman Church. Furthermore, a man most revered and indeed most renowned for his knowledge and way of life, Cardinal of Sant'Angelo in the Holy Roman Church, at that time also a pseudo-cardinal and ensnared in great error, grew radiant at the eloquence of such a virgin.[41] Raising his hands toward heaven, he said to the blessed Ursulina, "I swear by God and all the saints, you have attained the grace of salvation for us, just as the liberation of Jerusalem was entrusted to holy Judith."[42] When they heard this, some of the pseudo-cardinals, persisting most wickedly in their previously planned treachery and attitude toward the Holy Roman Church and not at all dislodged by Ursulina's arguments from the gross and deceitful errors of their ways, bore ill these words of the antipope and the gentle cardinal of Sant'Angelo. Not in words but with frowns, furrowed brows, and altered expressions they gave signs of their utter perfidy. Through careful artifice and premeditated plotting, they ensured that under no conditions would the blessed virgin Ursulina be able to have further access to the antipope or the cardinal of Sant'Angelo.

24a.[43] The utterly wicked pseudo-Cardinal Martin, more monstrous than the others, proved unable to cloak his faithlessness

---

41. This was William Noellet, named cardinal deacon of Sant'Angelo by Pope Gregory XI in 1371, who defected from the newly established Roman papacy of Urban VI, having participated in both the elections of 1378. He died soon after the incident described here. See Valois, *La France et le Grand Schisme*, 1:1–75, passim, and 2:360. William's career was notably international: he also served in the 1370s as archdeacon of Suffolk in the English diocese of Norwich: *Fasti Ecclesiae Anglicanae, 1300–1541: Monastic Cathedrals* (Southern Province) comp. B. Jones, vol. 4 of *Fasti Ecclesiae Anglicanae, 1300–1541*, ed. John Le Neve (London: Institute of Historical Research, 1962–67), 33.

42. In the Biblical book named after her, Judith saves the Jewish nation from its enemies, especially the Assyrian general Holofernes, whom she enchants with her charms and then beheads. Judith's pure physical courage finds an echo in Ursulina's.

43. The Latin edition has two sections numbered 24, which we have labeled 24a and 24b.

in silence.[44] Like a rabid dog, a ferocious lion, or a most savage and ravenous wolf, Martin contrived to entangle the blessed virgin Ursulina—or rather, the wisdom of the Holy Spirit—in his sophistries and supercilious speeches. With angry expression and flowery discourse, he said to her, "So: if you allege that you have come to us as the Lord's messenger, and furthermore have had as many revelations from Him as is reported, then explain the problem I'm about to present. I want you first of all to say explicitly what the Trinity is."[45] The blessed Ursulina, instructed by the Holy Spirit, tossed Martin into the trap he had set for her with a brilliant reply. "Did you ever see this Trinity that you so much want to know about? And if by chance you were to see it, would you recognize it?" Martin answered, "No, not at all." The blessed virgin said to him, "Therefore any disquisition I might make concerning the Trinity would be in vain, for you would not grasp it by such means." Having heard this reply, Martin desisted from his prattling and grew silent. Beaten in the first round of the fight, like a wily snake he readied another snare for the blessed virgin, but the serpent succumbed to the same weapon as the lion.[46] The great snake Martin spewed out something like this from his poisonous heart: "Since you speak personally with God—well, tell me, I say, enlighten me further, would you, please?—who are reckoned among the saved, and who among the damned?"[47] Reader, hear the blessed Ursulina's utterly elegant and sharp reply. She said to Martin, "Have you ever seen a tree adorned with the flowers it has brought forth?" After he replied that he had indeed, she replied, "Say I bring such a tree in to you. You're able in that case to tell the blooms that will produce good fruit from those that will come to nothing?" The pseudo-cardinal and his co-conspirators stood there without a clue how to reply. Ursulina

44. Affò, *Vita della Beata Orsolina*, 26, n. 1, mistakenly identifies this Martin as the bishop of Lisbon. But Martin of Lisbon died in 1383 and the only other Avignon cardinal of that name is Martin de Salvis, the bishop of Pamplona, elected cardinal in 1390: *Hierarchia Catholica Medii Aevi*, 2nd ed. (Monasterii: Libraria Regensbergiana, 1913–78), 1:27.

45. The nature and meaning of the Trinity was one of the most complicated and controversial aspects of Christianity from its origins in the ancient Mediterranean. It is no wonder Martin starts with a question on a subject that might easily reveal a heterodox or even heretical understanding on the part of his interlocutor—a trap, as Zanacchi calls it in the next sentence.

46. Martin is thus compared to the lions to whom Daniel was thrown after he prayed faithfully and the serpent whose wiles ended mankind's sojourn in Eden.

47. Again, Martin poses a question that had given rise to over a thousand years of controversy—and would become central in the Protestant Reformation of the sixteenth century.

finished by noting that knowledge of such matters is fitting only for God and those to whom he reveals it.

24b. Seeing themselves beaten by the blessed Ursulina, her enemies gnashed their teeth. Since they had been unable to defeat her in such conversation, they tried instead to overcome her with threats and haughty speeches. "Do you really believe," they enquired, "that you alone are more knowledgeable than all these cardinals and that you are wiser than these men who, since they have declared this to be the Catholic faith, do not for a second hesitate to die in that faith?" Replied Ursulina, "As God is my witness, I acknowledge that I do not, as a humble little female of minimal worth, think myself wiser than other people. But I have spoken to you as an instrument of the Holy Spirit." When they alleged that she had been prompted by others, she replied, "Your belief is in vain, for the things you just heard were not in the least taught to me by others."[48] In the end, the cardinals, judging that Ursulina's mother was the author of all these thoughts, separated the two women. They placed the mother in a monastery but handed over the blessed Ursulina to the care of a certain noble citizen's wife. That way their opportunity to speak to her could be granted them more easily and conveniently.[49] Tirelessly they lingered day and night, like rabid dogs, so that they might be able to lay some charge against the blessed virgin, truthfully or at least plausibly, and then—so they hoped—to scheme more evilly against her. But with God's help, Ursulina answered every harangue with all wise discretion, such that whether defeated, confounded, or silenced by her, they were always forced to desist. And when they tried to overcome or shatter the blessed virgin, sometimes with threats, sometimes with fright and fear, her face never changed and her expression never betrayed terror. So the men were never able to catch her faltering with uncertain words.

25. But these blind men, deprived of the grace of the True Light, were in no way changed for the better by the kindly virgin's holy example. Instead, they increased their treachery every day. Capable

---

48. Here again arises the question of discernment of spirits, as discussed in detail in the preface to the *Revelations* of Constance of Rabastens. To quote one scholar, in the world of late-medieval holy women, "Supernatural gift, diabolical illusions, and fakery intertwined in a climate of intense mysticism where ecstasies were considered the fullest form of communication with the divine" (Zarri, "Living Saints," 238).

49. More easily, that is, than if she were in a convent like her mother or than if they could harass her only in the papal palace, where Ursulina had some sympathizers like Peter of Puy and William Noellet. As is clear in section 28, Clement VII was unaware of the continued campaign against Ursulina.

of thinking of nothing but earthly matters, they wondered if perhaps the blessed Ursulina was making use of some magical or superstitious art, for they easily recognized that the virgin's eloquence exceeded human ability. Therefore, they made her change all her clothes and had them examined with minute and diligent care lest something shameful or suspicious were sewn up in some part of her garments.[50] They could not overcome or defeat this blessed virgin by crafty design or by means of shock, fright, threats, or anything else they contrived. They did not fear to afflict her with the rack and other savage tortures in order that she would say—this is what these utterly wicked people hoped for—that they were being overcome on all fronts by witchcraft. She declared, "I make no use of devilish witchcraft. I put into action the favor of Our Lord Jesus Christ for the salvation of your souls."

26. O you sinners, cruel agents of such wickedness! With what expressions, minds, and feelings, with what deliberate planning could you succeed in laying your evil hands on the blessed virgin? How could you put aside all awe and abandon the fear of God in whose stead you professed to act on earth and stir up your minds to make them overflow with pride, proffering the most monstrous words imaginable? And for what, I ask you, cruelest of creatures, did this holy, blessed virgin pray? Was it not the salvation of your souls? Whence came your hatefulness and gross impiety? From what source did your immense savagery flow, so great that you did not fear to exchange faith for faithlessness, sympathy for treachery, and hatred for love? Shame, shame! When they had led the blessed Ursulina to the rack, covered in the lowly sack they had put on her after taking her own clothes, these foulest of ministers labored to tie Ursulina's hands, bound behind her back, to the rack's ropes. But behold, the room in which they were carrying out the torture was shaken violently. Almost the entire structure of the house lay in ruin, threatening the collapse of the latest plan for Ursulina's destruction. When those present saw what was happening, they were stricken with abject terror. "Stop," they cried, "we must stop, lest we suffer the fate of those who tortured St. Catherine."[51] Moved by panic rather than love, they released the

---

50. The cardinals were searching for some kind of magical charm or talisman.

51. St. Catherine of Alexandria, according to legend a martyr of the last round of Christian persecutions in the early fourth century AD, had a story similar in some ways to Ursulina. She talked back to authorities—in Catherine's case the Emperor Maximus, whom she told to stop the persecutions—and confounded intellectual authorities, fifty pagan philosophers. She was sentenced die by means of a wheel set with spikes or razors, now known as "St.

blessed Ursulina unharmed. Grieving more for their damnation than the injuries they had done her, the blessed virgin said, "Since you have failed to keep faith as I told you to, expect divine judgment even before my departure."

27. They all marveled at her thoughtfulness and deliberation with everyone in every situation. The advocate Lord Anthony of Milan replied, "You would marvel in another way if you saw her working and dictating."[52] "I'd like to see that," replied the anticardinal Martin. They placed her in a hall, amidst four anticardinals and in the sight of a crowd. The blessed Ursulina, instructed by the Holy Spirit, began to sew and prophesy. Lord Anthony wrote down things that actually happened afterward. Hearing such words, all witnessing this spectacle were afraid, but nonetheless they did not yield in their malevolence on this account. Persisting in their obstinacy, they plotted day and night for seven months for the death of the blessed virgin. She was taken back to the first house, where they forced poison on her, first in drink and then in unguents, so that she might thereby know her last day. Signs of both kinds of poisoning were quite evident to those who saw her.[53] He, too, was a witness, the One who in his clemency freed her from all the designs of wicked people with his marvelous and ineffable kindness. In the end, once every threat and peril for deterring and exterminating the blessed virgin had been carried out and none of them worked—since never can any plan against the Lord or his servants succeed—for a while her enemies ceased surveillance and molestation of the blessed Ursulina. Far from content, they were exhausted and without further plans—more defeated, though, than pacified.

28. While they raged savagely against Ursulina in multifarious ways, the aforementioned antipope inquired about her and they replied that the silly fool had long since departed. This was soon reported to

---

Catherine's wheel," frequently depicted in Christian art. When Catherine was placed upon its rim, the wheel broke apart and the spikes flew off, killing onlookers. Witnesses to Ursulina's torture feared a similar fate.

52. The situation appears to be that while concentrating on domestic handiwork, Ursulina begins to recite marvels to be written down by someone else. See above, section 9, on dictation. Anthony of Milan, named in section 9 as one of Ursulina's scribes, is there called *procurator Clementis antipapae*, here simply *advocator*. The first title suggests fiscal responsibility, the second legal expertise. Anthony's service to Clement, whatever its exact nature, is not known to have been rewarded with the office of bishop or cardinal.

53. That is, poison applied internally and externally. The latter is described as *lotio capitis*, some kind of shampoo or unguent.

the blessed virgin, who at once dispatched the apostolic letter that she had held back by divine dispensation, the one she had brought from the supreme pontiff and his cardinals in Rome, addressed to Clement himself.[54] The antipope was quite astonished to learn that Ursulina had not left Avignon. When he read the letter, he was thunderstruck. Shaking his head, he stood motionless, sighing, troubled, pondering matters over for a long time. A few days later, this antipope Clement, washing his hands before sitting down to dine and preoccupied with the thought of sudden death, made a sorry end to his life.[55] So was fulfilled the prophecy of the blessed Ursulina: before death these wicked men would have a foreboding of divine judgment on their souls. Then Pedro de Luna took the previously mentioned letter and went off to Paris in order to consult with learned men about it.[56] But the other pseudo-cardinals, contemplating the blessed virgin's life, character, holiness, and steadfastness, underwent a change of heart. Greatly ruing the injuries they had inflicted on her, they had her led before them and asked the blessed Ursulina what they should do to obtain divine forgiveness for the wrongs done to her. She replied, "For the salvation of your souls and those of other people, you must submit at once, in harmony and concord, to the holy Roman Church." They all promised that they would fulfill the prayers of the blessed virgin and at once sent off a formal embassy to Pope Boniface in the hopes of obtaining God's mercy. As the departing ambassadors reached the city gates, that most ardent Enemy of all good works, full of ambition and a snake's wisdom, together with his basest servant, Pedro de Luna, newly returned with the advice of the masters of Paris, put an end to the pseudo-cardinals' soul-saving plan—just at the moment everything had been prepared and arranged for submission to the supreme pontiff. At once they recalled the ambassadors, elected Pedro de Luna as antipope, and declared that they would persist in the treacheries

---

54. See section 21.

55. On September 16, 1394.

56. Pedro de Luna, born in northern Spain in 1328, studied and later taught canon (church) law at Montpellier, in southern France. Pope Gregory XI appointed him cardinal deacon in 1375. At first an adherent of Gregory's Roman successor Urban VI, he later helped to elect and energetically served the Avignon pope Clement VII as an ambassador in his native Iberia. Later he was a legate to France, Brabant, Flanders, Scotland, England, and Ireland, spending much time in Paris among the learned men he consulted about Ursulina in 1394.

already begun.[57] Oh good Jesus, to whom all hearts are open, to whom every person's will is known, and from no secret is hidden,[58] did you perhaps change their minds because their conversion to the good was not fittingly humble? Or had they in their already deep-rooted evil presumed too much against divine will? I do not know. Nobody is a sharer in such a decision except you.

29. The blessed Ursulina, seeing that her enemies had returned to the error of their ways and feeling hopeless, returned home in her mother's company. After a few days' time she left Parma at the Lord's command, made for Rome, and soberly recounted to the pope all that had happened. She was received by Boniface with delight and joyful spirit. He took great pity on her for the many and diverse tribulations she endured in Avignon in the service of restoring Catholic faith. He offered himself obligingly to her, furthermore conferring numerous favors, namely fourteen privileges and grants, according to which she was permitted to build an oratory in her own home, and have the divine offices and Mass celebrated there, and several other things I think it best not to mention now.[59] At last, she returned home. When she had stayed there only a little while, at divine command she departed for Milan and approached its duke, then called the Count of Virtues, revealing to him many of God's secrets for the honor and preservation of his position.[60] But in no way did he want to bend his ears when the blessed Ursulina began this way: "Unless you believe my words, since indeed they are God's prophecies, know that you will suffer great persecutions and tribulations in short order"—which

---

57. Pedro de Luna was elected pope in Avignon on September 28, 1394, taking the name of Benedict XIII. Despite Zanacchi's rhetoric, Pedro/Benedict claimed to be a firm advocate of reuniting the Church, by means of his own resignation if necessary. However, during many years of complex intrigue he never ceded the title, even after the Council of Constance ended the schism for good in 1417. He died in his native Aragon some years later, in extreme old age, among a few cardinals who remained loyal to the end.

58. These phrases are a part of the liturgy of the Mass, a prayer for purity.

59. Zanacchi shows the same concern he attributed to Ursulina herself in section 10, above: the dangers of appearing to be excessively spiritual, especially for women.

60. This was Duke Gian Galeazzo Visconti (1351–1402), who won over to Milanese control many major cities of northern Italy (Parma had been under Milanese lordship since 1347). The sobriquet "Count of Virtues" was a pun based on his having obtained land around Vertùs, east of Paris, as part of the dowry of his first wife, princess Isabelle, daughter of King John II of France. Milan is about 70 miles northwest of Parma, so this destination was, at long last, not too far from Ursulina's home.

came about through the condottiere Facino Cane.[61] Among other things, the blessed virgin ordered that the Duke take up the defense of the Catholic faith, and that he should in no way interfere in church teachings.

30. This blessed virgin, after numerous labors and hardships in her many journeys made at divine command, decided to visit the holy tomb of our Lord Jesus Christ and other sites of His Holy Passion. She went to the famed city of Venice along with her mother, where there was a great number of ships bound for those holy places. When she had arrived and learned that a certain very trustworthy vessel would weigh anchor in two or three months, she decided to arrange passage on it since its departure schedule was convenient.[62] Meanwhile Ursulina returned to Rome and visited the holy places there. When she had spent only a few days, having received the blessing of the pope, leaving Rome she went to Urbino. There she was detained three days by the vows and prayers of certain venerable ladies; they spoke of God, passing their time in the worship of Christ.[63] Leaving Urbino, she re-entered the aforesaid city of Venice accompanied by her mother. They discovered that the ship they had chosen had set sail on their chosen itinerary two days earlier.[64] Her mother took this very badly and said

---

61. Although Gian Galeazzo suffered a few defeats in the years after he met Ursulina, he was in fact an extremely successful warrior. His general Facino Cane appears never to have rebelled against Gian Galeazzo, but he was an important figure in the machinations and rebellions that followed the duke's premature death in 1402, leaving two young sons who could not hold their father's territory together. As Affò suggests, it would have been easy for Zanacchi to make this anachronistic error over seventy years later (Affò, *Vita della Beata Orsolina*, 34, n. 2).

62. Venice, a commercial port city on the northern Adriatic Sea, is about 150 miles' journey from Parma. Ursulina probably set off in late 1395. Venice and Genoa were the most popular ports for departure on pilgrimage and especially in Venice, all-inclusive package tours were offered to pilgrims. These included the passage, meals, a boat to go on shore en route, protection from the oarsmen, rooms to keep poultry, and of course guided tours of the main attractions. It is most likely a trip of this sort that Ursulina booked for herself, her mother, and probably others, since the pope's bull permitting her trip (translated in the Appendix) mentions that ten others had permission to accompany the mother and daughter. See Chareyron, *Pilgrims to Jerusalem in the Middle Ages*, 41–46 on "the Venetian Tourist Office" and 42–43 for a detailed contract issued to the famous German pilgrim Felix Fabri in 1483.

63. Urbino is a city near the Adriatic coast, northeast of Rome across the peninsula. Since the text does not identify the women Ursulina joined in prayers, it seems probable that they were pious laywomen.

64. The round-trip journey from Venice to Rome and back via Urbino is at some 600 miles, depending on the route, which would have meant almost constant travel across a few

to the blessed Ursulina, "If you had not tarried with those ladies, we would have arrived in time to board a good, new ship. Now it is gone and we are forced to take an old one." The blessed Ursulina replied, "It is divine disposition. Be happy, Mother, and do not be grieved at the will of God: know that this happened by God's command."

31. Directing her feet toward a very old ship, Ursulina went on board. When it put its sails to the blowing winds of the deep and cleaved the Adriatic along a favorable route in mid-sea, the passengers saw a boulder a ways off from the ship. The sailors, moved by great pity, began to weep, saying among themselves, "Alas! A few days ago the ship that left Venice a little ahead of us, laden with so many men and women bound in devotion for the Holy Land, was seized by howling winds and pushed along by a very strong storm. Tossed by whirlpools this way and that, it hit that rock and suffered completely destructive shipwreck. What a miserable catastrophe! Nobody got off that ship alive." When she had heard these things, Bertolina understood clearly that God, the wisest director of all things, watched over and guided her and the blessed virgin Ursulina. Accordingly, the mother conducted herself more wisely with her daughter and gave God thanks for the danger averted by means of the delay among the venerable ladies of Urbino. The blessed Ursulina, since she suffered terrible nausea and vomiting from the unaccustomed movement of the ocean, did not doubt in the slightest that she was approaching the way of all flesh; she asked God for a grace period of fifteen years, just as Hezekiah had done.[65] And so it happened, as was clear at her death.

32. At last favorable winds blew, and after a safe journey Ursulina landed at the hoped-for holy places. She began to visit them as time allowed with all the devotion placed in the holy and silent treasure-chest of her heart. Of course, nobody except God, the searcher of hearts, could imagine how many tears and sighs she poured forth at that holiest of stables where the Savior himself deigned to be born.[66] Nor could anyone else know how many prayers she interrupted with bitter sobbing when she thought piously that the God-made-

---

months. It is no wonder Ursulina and her mother missed their ship's departure.

65. Hezekiah was a king of Judah, one of two kingdoms that emerged after the division of Solomon's united kingdom of Israel. During a grave illness, he prayed to God, who granted him another fifteen years to live as a reward for his faithfulness (2 Kgs 20:1–7). On the fifteen years, see section 36, below.

66. That is, the first stop on Ursulina's pilgrimage was Bethlehem, a town just south of Jerusalem said in the Gospels to be the birthplace of Jesus.

man had given forth his first cries there and showed with many proofs that he would be a true man.[67] She pondered how in that place ox and ass recognized their God, the Maker of all creation, and she feasted inwardly on each and every act that had taken place there, with calm mind, sweet meditation, and honeyed savor. Next she proceeded to the site of the crucifixion (that is, the greatest mystery of our redemption), anxious and overwhelmed with thirsty desire to see the place.[68] There her happy soul—now happier[69]—her holy head, her sweet-dripping heart dissolved in crying and sighing, groaned prayers, poured forth tears copiously, and put forth heaving sobs. She divided up and feasted upon every piece of Our Lord Jesus Christ's passion and death, and by such deep meditation exhausted all the strength of her body.[70] When she had visited every one of the most holy places and tasted, as we said, the mysteries of each, she had a peaceful voyage back to Venice, whence she had come. Staying there for many days in most saintly fashion, she turned many to holiness and established many good customs to the point that she was venerated by all as if a saint. Her renown and holiness still thrive in Venice today.

33.   Afterwards Ursulina went home. Back in Parma, for quite some time she thought over in the silent counsel of her holy breast what she had seen and caressed and so piously tasted. O sacred head and happiest of souls! Many times she fully recalled her own abundant tears and interrupted sobs, and many times she renewed those sweetest of sighs and groans. She renewed many sweet and concerned sorrows with hands clasped, then crossed, and sometimes spread out toward heaven, her eyes cast down. Thus with such most holy meditations, sweetest of thoughts, and honeyed bitterness she urged forth and cheerfully struck her holy heart and modest mind. To tell the truth, what is sweeter than this contemplation? What is gentler, or more pleasant to see, or more delightful to touch than to recall that there the Lord Jesus was born, suffered, and buried for us, or to meditate on the site of our redemption and release from

---

67. According to Catholic orthodoxy established in the fourth century, Jesus was both fully divine and fully human.

68. Ursulina has now reached Jerusalem.

69. Since her soul has since proceeded to its eternal reward in heaven.

70. Profound bodily experience of religious devotion and physicality of religious ecstasy were typical of late-medieval Christian spirituality; the next section continues its emphasis on the corporeal aspect of Ursulina's post-pilgrimage meditations. Again, Zanacchi stresses the orthodoxy of the unusual Ursulina.

miserable captivity, or to touch with one's own hands the holes of the cross and the cracks in the rocks?[71] Who, while thinking about, seeing, and touching these things could hold back a flood of tears? Who, I say, is so iron-like, terrible, and cruel? I believe that nobody could leave the Holy Land dry-eyed, without sorrow and sighing, or lacking in devotion. In that place every iron mind and wicked heart would immediately put aside its savagery. What human tongue could say or heart contemplate what this blessed woman, totally happy in her soul, said and thought there? None, evidently. Therefore, I have deliberately decided that these matters should be passed over in silence, lest by some chance, in understating I should unintentionally slander the outstanding virgin.[72]

34. Meanwhile, as the blessed virgin feasted on such nourishment in her homeland, Ottobono Terzi ruled there in Parma along with Lord Pietro Rossi after the death of Gian Galeazzo Visconti, the duke of Milan, called the Count of Virtues.[73] But when disagreement arose between Ottobono and Pietro, the former prevailed and massacred many of his opponent's party. For this reason he was considered by many to be outside the realm of humanity, a concocter of every savagery and creator of barbarity. Satan, that murderer of serenity, put it in his mind to shake the blessed virgin, her mother, and a great part of the citizenry from their peace and quiet, for the Enemy was jealous of her peacefulness.[74] Summoning Bertolina, Ottobono told her and others that if from that day they were found in the city, he would not hesitate to burn them alive. This cruel tyrant ordered that a two-penny candle be lit and set up next to the town bell in the middle of the street; when it was burnt down, whoever was still found within the city would be put to the sword. When Bertolina heard this, she marveled much more that Ottobono had set a deadline than at what she had been ordered to do. For he was such a worker of savagery against all that he never hesitated or granted a stay of execution for anyone who had offended him in the slightest, but immediately acted

71. According to Matthew 27:51, a great rock-splitting earthquake accompanied the death of Jesus; pilgrims in Jerusalem visited fissures said to have been created at that time.

72. Here as elsewhere, Zanacchi's account is very much what Ursulina said and did rather than what she thought: it is her actions that speak of her consciousness and her interior life.

73. See notes 60 and 61. After Gian Galeazzo's death in 1402, several northern Italians cities fell into the hands of his generals: Ottobono Terzi took over in Parma.

74. On Ursulina's place in the factional politics of Parma, see the introduction to this volume.

to carry out the desire of his cruel will. Nobody attributed this delay to such a fierce man having found some scrap of humanity, but rather to divine mercy invoked by the unceasing prayers and vows of the blessed virgin Ursulina.

35. The blessed Ursulina and her mother wanted to give wide berth to such a tyrant since the highest Truth himself had said: If you are persecuted in one city, flee to another.[75] They left their homeland and went to Bologna.[76] There Ursulina served her bridegroom Jesus Christ for a little while in all humility, with perpetual prayer, many vigils, numerous fasts, incessant subjection, and most plentiful meditation. From Bologna she set forth in the company of Lady Maristella, abbess of the house of San Paulo in Parma, who had also been expelled by the tyrant and had often seen the virgin lifted a cubit off the ground, when the Lord was showing her in a vision the creation of the first man.[77] Along with Maristella and Bertolina, she went to Verona.[78] There, with her aid and effort, God himself, the builder of all good things, contrived that a certain monastery of nuns—which Satan had long since completely stripped of all good living and order—recover, return, and revert to its former holiness of regular observance and regular manner of life.[79] The blessed Ursulina lived three years in Verona, nearly unknown, or at least nobody knew of her outstanding merit in God's eyes, although she was believed to be of praiseworthy life and repute among other matrons.[80] Seeking food and shelter for herself by her own hands, along with her mother she begged for her modicum of nourishment.[81] However, in each moment she suckled on

75. Matthew 10:23. This is part of Jesus' instructions to his twelve apostles, whom he warns to expect persecution.

76. Bologna is 50 miles southeast of Parma.

77. This is the only mention of a supernatural bodily manifestation of Ursulina's visions: see the introduction. The nunnery dedicated to St. Paul in Parma was founded in the early eleventh century by the local bishop. On Abbess Maristella, see the introduction.

78. Verona, where Ursulina ended her travels, is about 70 miles north of Bologna.

79. Zanacchi does not identify this house, but there were several communities of religious women in and around Verona. Once more, Zanacchi stresses a most orthodox holy activity, the reformation of a monastic house and its restoration to regular life, that is, one ordered by a written rule (*regula*).

80. These women might have been nuns, who had heard about her monastic reform, or perhaps pious laywomen like those Ursulina had known in Urbino.

81. This account makes it sound as if Ursulina and Bertolina (and Maristella?) were reduced to penury and mendicancy. On one hand, this was a humiliation and a trial for members of the prosperous urban middle class from which Ursulina came. On the other hand, it is also

the richness of the Holy Spirit and the Holy Scripture and the fat of meditations; in this way she tended to her most happy soul and calm mind with divine food.

36. Our Lord God Jesus Christ, the most generous rewarder of all honorable works, wanting to make the blessed Ursulina a co-heir and sharer in his celestial kingdom and confer a prize for her prayers, vigils, self-discipline, fasting, all her labors, and her immense love, visited a great sickness on her body. When the illness grew graver, the blessed virgin's mother said to her, "I beg you, my daughter, and again I plead with you, ask the Lord for relief of your condition. Come, my daughter, I beg you: do as I hope, act as I ask, seek what I so very much desire. Do not let me be orphaned of your very pleasing company, child. I plead with you, daughter, have pity on your mother, take mercy on the grief of the womb that bore you." Bertolina copiously assailed her daughter with such words. The blessed virgin replied, "We must bear God's will with equanimity, mother, for God knows what we need. Did God lead us into this wicked and miserable world for nothing? Did we not bear a portion of our cross? Woe is me! Is it not necessary that we guilty ones suffer along with Christ, our head? For we are his body.[82] He, although innocent, suffered to free us from most shameful death so that by His mercy, we could fly away to the heavenly homeland along with Him. Know now, dearest mother, and you brothers and sisters standing with us, that I have entered on the way of all flesh, and I must render to our mother earth what is hers. Now the fifteenth year is completed since I thought myself near death in the ship and sought a fifteen-year extension of my life from the Lord.[83] Therefore, it remains that you and I together submit ourselves to the yoke of divine will. This is a particularly Christian act and a sign of a soul destined for eternal glory."

37. Then the Reverend Lady Maristella, Abbess of San Paulo, whom we mentioned earlier, said to the blessed virgin Ursulina, "I beg you, and I bear witness through your bridegroom the Lord Jesus, who

---

an imitation of Christ, himself a homeless wanderer; poverty for religion's sake was a major theme of Christian life in the later Middle Ages.

82. Christ as the head of the church whose members are its body is a standard medieval metaphor.

83. See section 31. Unsurprisingly, given that this *vita* provides only one date, that of the subject's birth, Zanacchi's chronology is confused: this fifteen-year extension must have happened earlier, most likely during her first trip to Avignon, since Affò argues convincingly that Ursulina died in 1408: *Vita della Beata Orsolina*, 45–48.

is the greatest love and affection, and who is our Lord in common: tell us if in your weakness God himself has made you a sharer in the glory of paradise." The blessed virgin Ursulina, filled with all humility, overflowing with great love, knowing that in a short time she would return her happy soul to God, is said to have given this response in all wholesomeness. "God, to whom be all honor and glory, and to whom all our purpose should be directed, with His great and ineffable kindness never ceased, once he began, to make me, His servant, a sharer in His great goodness. He never failed to water poor and unworthy me with the dew of his kindness, fully and at length every day, and he has fed me with this sort of grace right up until now." Bertolina, now more certain from these words of her daughter's imminent passing, was on one hand filled with joy, since she had no doubt that the blessed Ursulina would ascend to the heavenly homeland of Jerusalem, but on the other hand was troubled by great sadness that she would be deprived of such a consolation and strong staff for her old age in this world. Nevertheless, choking down her tears and with forced joy on her face, she said to her daughter, "I beg you, my sweet daughter, whom I bore from my womb and nursed on my own milk, that before you ascend to the supernal city, leave me and these others standing by some memorial of yourself for the salvation of our souls." The blessed Ursulina responded, "I first beg that you love one another. Next: keep a true and lively faith, holding it certain that whatever might happen to you proceeds entirely from God on account of the immense love he has for his creation, not hate. Finally I exhort and leave to you each as a memorial, that you should never condemn any person by your own judgment." For the holy virgin knew how deceitful, by its very nature, the judgment of men and our souls is; indeed it is a most lethal poison derived from our own fragility.

38. Afterwards, when Bertolina and the women there with her thought that the blessed Ursulina was about to depart from this world and had, according to custom, lit candles around her, she realized what was happening and said to those around her, "You labor in vain over my funeral, for the end will be tomorrow." Meanwhile, the Lord showed her many astonishing signs concerning the damnation and salvation of different ranks of people, that is, Christians, Saracens, and Jews, that I saw and read with my own eyes.[84] Finally, in her last illness she was racked with fevers and extraordinary abdominal pain,

---

84. "Saracen" is a common medieval description of Muslims. Here again, Zanacchi refers to materials concerning details of Ursulina's life that have not survived.

so weakened and wasted that she could properly be thought not a human creature but a heavenly one, nurtured by divine inspiration and showing all a miracle in herself. Nevertheless, she was calm of countenance, with cheerful expression, and nothing else resounded from her holy mouth except "Oh my Jesus, my Jesus!" Her fortitude was marvelous and amazing; there could be no doubt that it was a gift of God, who works miraculously through His saints and is proclaimed wondrous. "Will my soul," says David, "not be subject to God? From him comes my strength [Ps 61/62:1(2)]." Then Ursulina is said to have poured forth a prayer to God. "Oh eternal God, oh greatest master, you made and shaped this vessel of corporeal creation from the clay of the earth. Oh sweetest love! Oh burning affection, that you made this vessel from such filth and yet put in it so great and grand a treasure, the soul, which bears the image of you, eternal God. You are my good master, my sweet love. You are that master, who builds and rebuilds, who breaks and makes whole again this vessel according to the pleasure of your goodness. I, your wretched servant, again offer you, eternal Father, my life, which I commend to you, highest One, for the reform of your sweet and delightful bride, Holy Mother Church. Have mercy, Lord and eternal Father, and pardon me for the great ignorance and still greater neglect with which I offended your bride, the Church: I did not do as I should have. I have sinned. Lord, have mercy on me and grant me, I beg, your blessing. Amen."

39. After these words she struck her breast many times, saying, "*Mea culpa*, eternal Trinity, that I have wretchedly offended your majesty with great carelessness, disobedience, ingratitude, ignorance, and many other failings. Oh, miserable me, for I have observed neither your general commands nor those made particularly to me by your goodness and most of all your instruction to me that I always pay you honor and labor for my fellow Christians. But I did the opposite, because I sought honor for myself and in time of need I shunned work for my fellow man. *Mea culpa*, Lord, for you taught me, Father, that I should forsake and lose myself wholly and seek only the praise and honor of your name, for the salvation of souls, with the longing for taking food at the table of your Holy Cross. But I sought my own consolation and was not zealous to see souls in the hands of their lords.[85] You, most merciful Father, often summoned me to embrace you with fire-tested and loving desire, with the heart's tears, with humble, constant, and

---

85. Since *Dominus*, Lord, is the title of priests entrusted with providing sacraments for religious women, perhaps the reference is to them.

faithful prayer, for the salvation of the whole world and the reform of Holy Mother Church, your sweetest bride, promising manifestly to renew that spouse. But I, a wretch, never replied, and slept away in the bed of my neglect—and therefore so many great evils came into the world and such ruination to your bride the Church. Alas for pitiful me! I did not regard your countless gifts with due reverence, nor see the blessings of the sweetest torments and punishments that you inflicted on this fragile body. Woe is me! I did not respect the indescribable love and honor with which you gave me these gifts and therefore I did not receive them with love and fiery desire. Woe is me! My sweet love, eternal spouse of my soul, you chose me as your bride from my youth, and I was not faithful to you, but a faithless adulteress, since I did not wholly remember you and your highest of blessings and thus my will was not well disposed to love and follow you as you asked me."[86] Ursulina, this purest dove, spoke of her guilt in these and many other matters, often beating her breast as an example to others.

40. These things finished, she received the sacraments of the Church with humble devotion and reverence. Afterwards, she fixed the eyes of her body on a picture of the Crucified One and began to pray devoutly and speak so loudly that she could hardly be understood. Then, her mother was summoned and Ursulina said to her, "Sweetest mother, I seek a blessing for your daughter, whom you bore, for it is time I return to Him who sent me. Behold, my spouse calls me: the time and the hour I predicted to you is at hand." Then her mother, weeping in the narrow space of her heart, said with all modest devotion, "Take pity, my daughter, on your mother, take pity on the womb that bore you and on the breasts that nursed you. Where are you going, daughter? Woe is me! Where are you leaving me? Blessed be you, daughter, but I beg that you also bless your grieving mother." Then the blessed Ursulina, lifting her hand a little, gave a blessing to her mother and others at her bedside, saying, "Lord, you call me and behold, I am coming to you. I come not by my own merits, but by your mercy's intervention, which I ask from you by virtue of the blood of your son." Then she said quietly,

---

86. In this extraordinary prayer of self-condemnation and gratitude, Ursulina offers a confession of disobedience and negligence in the face of God's special guidance and plans for her. Particularly important—and characteristic of late medieval affective piety—is the intimacy of her terms: God is her husband and "sweet love" just as he is also the spouse of the earthly Church Ursulina castigates herself for not having sufficiently renewed. It had been many years since her journeys between Rome and Avignon, and still the Great Schism endured at Ursulina's death.

"Father, into your hands I commit my soul and my spirit."[87] In this sickness, indeed worn away with this martyrdom, Ursulina rested in a holy death. Leaving us in the body, she returned her soul to God to reign with him forever and ever. Amen.

41. Having died in this manner, the blessed Ursulina took up the promise that she had seen and greeted from afar, acknowledging herself a pilgrim and a stranger on earth: as the Apostle says, as long as we are in the body, we are in exile from the Lord [2 Cor 5:6]. Her holy little body remained unburied for three whole days, and on the third day it was so fresh, so beautiful, and so supple that she would have been thought not dead but sleeping. "You will not allow your holy one to see corruption," says David [Ps 15/16:10]. These words might have been spoken, albeit prophetically, concerning the Lord Jesus Christ, whose most holy flesh saw no corruption, as the holy apostle Peter witnesses in the Acts of the Apostles [Acts 2:30-32]. However, they can also be understood to apply to the venerable Ursulina and other saints, since they are Christ's members: For He, as the Apostle says, is our head [Col 1:18], with the whole body of the Church linked and united through every joint. Who, then, could fail to believe that this venerable and holy Ursulina, as a member of Christ, reigns with Him in the heavenly kingdom? Who could doubt she is a blessed one? Oh truly blessed Ursulina, thrice and four times blessed, behold: what you believed you now see, and what you yearned for you now have. Remember us, I beg, and help us, who are tossed in the storms of this world. With the intercession of your prayers draw us along behind you, so that we may run the course of life in the sweet smell of your virtues.[88]

42. But for all that, oh blessed virgin Ursulina, my mother[89] and most hearty advocate, let me not leave off here, instead proceeding according to the power of my small talent to tell with praises of the virtues with which you were always adorned: faith, hope, and love,

---

87. Ursulina echoes the words of Christ on the cross (Lk 23:46). The scene here is also reminiscent of the crucifixion as recounted in the Gospel of John, which emphasizes the presence of Jesus' mother Mary at her son's death (Jn 18: 25–27).

88. The notion of the "odor of sanctity," used chiefly in a sarcastic manner in modern English, was a very real and serious concept in the Middle Ages. Holy bodies were thought to emit a sweet smell.

89. On the use of "mother" to refer to holy women neither heads of nunneries, that is, mothers superior, nor biological mothers, see Laura A. Smoller, "Holy Mothers: The History of a Designation of Spiritual Status" in Marc R. Forster and Benjamin J. Kaplan, ed., *Piety and Family in Early Modern Europe* (Burlington: Ashgate, 2005), 178–200.

prudence, justice, fortitude, temperance, and humility.[90] This blessed virgin was so full of faith (without which it is impossible for anyone to please God) that like another Enoch she always walked with God in her mind [Gn 5:22]. In her faith she offered, not from the firstborn of his flock like Abel, but from her own self, the highest sacrifice to God, living, holy, and pleasing in its reasoned prayer [Gn 4:4]. Living in certainty, she expected herself to gain not this city remaining here on earth, but the future one, with its eternal foundations, whose founder and artisan is God.[91] In her faith imitating the example of the ancient Holy Fathers, she spurned the riches, honors, and pleasures of this world.[92] She considered those things as dung and chose to live in poverty, want, affliction, and toil so that she might be made a worthy companion of the saints in the heavenly homeland. In her faith, finally, she was made righteous, since she was always at peace with God. By her hope dedicated to heavenly good, like a daughter of God she gloried in all her tribulations, knowing that "tribulation gives rise to patience, patience to testing, and testing to hope [Rom 5:3–4]." Hope of this sort did not disturb her, for the love of God overspread her heart through the Holy Spirit that had been granted to her. Indeed she burned with love toward the Lord and her neighbors with a pure heart, good conscience, and true faith—with that love, I say, of which the holy Apostle says, "Love is patient and kind, love is not jealous and does not act wrongly, it is not puffed up or vainglorious, it does not seek its own advantage, it is not excited to anger, it does not plot evil. Love does not delight in wickedness, but rejoices in truth [1 Cor

90. In Catholic teaching, faith, hope, and charity are called the theological or spiritual virtues, derived from 1 Corinthians 13:13. They are of the soul and supernatural. Prudence, justice, fortitude, and temperance are the four cardinal Christian virtues, sometimes called natural virtues, derived from pre-Christian philosophical traditions; they are more rational and worldly. These seven were often collected as a list. To them, Zanacchi adds humility, usually considered to belong under the heading of temperance, as a special attribute of Ursulina. The rest of this section elaborates on Ursulina's theological virtues; the next treats her cardinal virtues more briefly.

   For the next several sections Zanacchi delivers a sermon-eulogy; the translation cites Biblical quotations or paraphrases in brackets, with more complex references discussed in notes.

91. Here Zanacchi refers to the formula of St. Augustine of Hippo (354–430), whose theology of history divided the universe into the ephemeral City of Man and the eternal City of God.

92. Zanacchi refers in particular to holy people of the third, fourth, and fifth centuries, who left the world and sought solitude and communion with God in the deserts of Egypt and elsewhere in the eastern Mediterranean.

13:4–6]." All these qualities were in the blessed virgin: she was patient and kind, envious of nobody, even the virtuous. Who ever saw her act wickedly? Pride and ambition were far distant from her. Not seeking her own advantage, but only that of Jesus Christ, she was most patient, never angered by insults or injuries. In no way plotting evil, she was saddened by wickedness and rejoiced in righteousness and truth.

43. But what shall I say about her prudence, justice, fortitude, and temperance? She was prudent in her actions, just in her guidance, strong in adversity, temperate in success. In her prudence, she knew what needed doing and prudently she chose what she ought and rejected what she ought. She enjoyed good fortune calmly and bore adversity with strength. Justly giving to each person his just desserts, she was so prudent that she never desired anything regrettable, nor did anything but what was just. She was so temperate that, fearing nothing except shamefulness, whatever she thought and did was guided by the rule of reason. She had such fortitude that not only did she curb earthly desires, but even wholly forgot about them. Finally, she was so just that, turning every thought of her soul to God alone, she saw Him, fixed in her mind's eye, as the beginning, middle, and end of all good things. What more can I say? Trained in a whole arsenal of virtues, like another Judith, Ursulina so strongly confounded and overcame the proud Holofernes and his whole army—that is, the Devil and all his vices—that worthily it can be sung of her, "God blessed you with his strength, because he reduced his enemies to nothing through you [Jdt 13:22]." You are the glory of your city of Parma, the joy of your people, the honor and fame of your race. You bring honor to all your daughters who emulate you. You fought like a man and your heart was strengthened such that you loved virtue and did not follow vice. Therefore, the hand of the Lord strengthened you and you will be blessed forever.[93] And so did not this most holy virgin, adorned with gems and precious stones, that is, distinguished by virtues of this sort, fully deserve to hear, when led into the bedchamber of her beloved Spouse, "You are wholly beautiful, my love, and flawless [Sg 4:7]"?

44. Therefore, Reverend Mother in Christ, and you, most devoted sisters in Christ,[94] let us be joyful and exult and give glory to God, we who have merited such an advocate and follower, who now, led into the bedchamber of the eternal king, ceaselessly pleads with

---

93. These last two sentences are a close paraphrase of the Israelites' praises of Judith: Judith 15: 10–11.

94. Zanacchi returns to direct address of the patrons and addressees of the whole *vita*.

God for our salvation and grace. Because of the value of her virtues, we are confident that nothing will be denied her. But it remains, my venerable and most beloved mothers in Christ, that in conclusion I exhort you with a son's boldness and love (although there is no need to do so) to be zealous in following the tracks of the aforementioned blessed virgin Ursulina along a righteous path. For she is a burning lamp, placed not under a bushel but atop a candelabra,[95] who gives light with the splendor of her virtues and the glint of her miracles, not just to us but also to all the faithful of God's house. This woman, I say, like a pillar leads you nuns forth from Egypt (that is, from worldly shadows and tribulations) and through the vast and terrible desert of this world toward the promised land flowing with milk and honey, as all the while you hope to reach the heavenly homeland with its heavenly city of Jerusalem, that is, the vision of peace; she is as a torch in this shadowy desert, offering you the light of discretion in the night of temptation and the consolation of refreshment in the heat of temptation.[96]

45. Your holy company is the sweetest-smelling evangelical country the Lord blessed [Gn 27:27]. It shows by which path each one of you should enter the bedchamber of the highest king, into which the most holy virgin Ursulina has already been led through her singular humility, the first virtue of Christians. For those who are true virgins and disciples of the Lord must walk just as Christ walked. For He taught his disciples and followers by word and example that this is the foundation of all virtues, as it were. He taught by word when he said, "Learn from me" ("not," as St. Augustine says, "to make the world, not to create all things visible and invisible, not to perform miracles in this world and raise the dead"[97]) but "because I am gentle and humble in my heart [Mt 11:29]." He taught by example since He is the son of God, God eternal, immense, and unfathomable, the maker of all things visible and invisible, descending from His Father's glory and his royal seat into this vale of tears, taking on human flesh from the womb of the humble and most blessed Virgin Mary, born

95. A saying of Jesus: see Matthew 5:15, Mark 4:21, and Luke 11:33.

96. This long and allusive sentence refers to the departure of the Hebrews, under the leadership of Moses, from Egypt (Ex 13:17–22). During the journey that would eventually lead them to the promised land of Israel, flowing with milk and honey, the Hebrews were led by God in a pillar of cloud during the daytime, a pillar of fire at night. So Ursulina, in her spiritual leadership of the nuns of San Quintino, has aspects of both God and Moses. Medieval Latin commentators often translated Jerusalem as "visio pacis," the vision of peace.

97. Augustine, Sermon 69, (PL 38: 441), a commentary on Matthew 11:28–29.

as a poor, small, lowly boy, living most humbly in the world for thirty years, who at last condescended in his humility to be arrested, beaten, crucified, and die for our redemption by his humble and base death on the cross. He humbled himself even unto death, death on the cross, says the Apostle [Phil 2:8]. There is no foundation better, more beneficial, or more salutary than the one the blessed Jesus Christ set in place—that is, humility, without which, as St. Gregory says, anyone who gathers other virtues is carrying dust into the wind and is all the more blinded by what he bears with him.[98] On this foundation, therefore, the house of all other virtues is constructed so that it reaches the height of love, which is God.

46. If, venerable and most beloved mothers, you want to be exalted, if you desire to enter into the sight of God, devote yourself to this foundation of humility, and upon it build for yourselves a tabernacle out of living stones, that is, other virtues, crafted not on earth but in heaven, spiritual and immortal. Emulate the venerable and holy virgin Ursulina, who devoted herself wholly to humility like a true disciple of the Lord Jesus Christ, her most kind spouse, whom she followed most humbly in mind and prayer through her whole life on earth and who in her abovementioned death gave you and other virgins an exemplar. Although the Apostle Paul says he has no teaching from the Lord concerning virgins, nevertheless he offers the opinion that it is good for them to remain in that state [1 Cor 7:25–26].[99] Then he adds that the unmarried woman or the virgin ponders godly things and how to please God and to be holy in body and spirit; she considers, he says, what are matters of God and not those of the world, not the things of men but of God [1 Cor 7:34]. Let her first consider, he says, how to please God, not simply men, since if, according to that same apostle, she strives to please men, she is not a servant of Christ [Gal 1:10].

47. St. Paul adds that a virgin should be holy in body and spirit. Holy in body, that is, that she keep holiness in all the parts of her body, since if there is rot in one part, there can be no holiness in the others. Therefore, in order that she be holy, let a virgin cleanse her head (for it is the chief member of the body) of all filth and worldly

98. Gregory the Great, Homily 7 (PL 76: 1103), a commentary on John 1:19–28. St. Gregory, pope from 590 to 604, was the last of the great Latin Doctors of the ancient world. Like St. Augustine, Gregory was frequently read and quoted in the Middle Ages.

99. The biblical language refers to men and women alike. Here and for the rest of the paragraph, Zanacchi is closely paraphrasing Paul, whose text he cites from memory.

adornments and vanities. Let her cleanse her neck, encircling it not
with gold jewelry but rather those ornaments of which Scripture says:
"Let mercy and truth never be absent from you; hang them around
your neck" [Prv 3:3]. Let her cleanse her eyes of all lustful desires,
since the holy prophet Jeremiah lamented, "My eye has robbed
my soul [Lam 3:51]." Let her cleanse her tongue of falsehood, for a
lying mouth kills the soul. Let her cleanse the mouth of murmuring,
criticism, and oaths, as it is written: Do not make any oaths but let
your words be "It is" and "It is not [Mt 5:34, 37]." Let her cleanse it
of frivolous and idle words, for we will be called upon to render an
account for every idle word on Judgment Day. Let her cleanse her ears
so that they listen only to holy and true discourse. And let her cleanse
her hands, so they are ready for all works of piety and mercy. Finally
let her cleanse her feet, so they may enter into the arduous and narrow
road that leads to heaven [Mt 7:14]. For the path that goes to heaven
is called the Sacred Way, as the prophet Isaiah says, and no polluted
virgin will pass along it [Is 35:8]. When the virgin has cleansed all her
body's members of every spot of sin, then let her know her virginity
will benefit her. Therefore let her body be holy but also her spirit, that
is, may she not allow any wicked deed into her thoughts. For that
virgin is as holy in body as in soul who sins not in body or mind, in
the knowledge that God is the examiner of the heart. Therefore, holy
virgins, I beg you to labor to cleanse your soul totally of sin, like your
body, for it is written: "Blessed are the pure in heart, for they will see
God [Mt 5:8]." Accordingly, I exhort you all as one, mothers, that you
be for all a model of pious living in Christ and a paradigm of virtues,
like the aforementioned venerable and blessed virgin Ursulina.

48. But now, most beloved and venerable mothers and sisters
in Christ, it is time for me to put an end to this my undertaking,
concerning which I fear rebuke because I have exceeded due measure
and been too presumptuous and rash. The duty of a monk, someone
says, is to lament and pray rather than use up time in the composition
of discourses of this kind.[100] Yet I call God, the examiner of the heart,
as my witness that I dictated this little work led neither by rashness nor
any presumption. Nothing but singular zeal of devotion impelled me
to it, along with the immense power of the love I had, have, and always
will have as long as I live both for you, my dearest and most venerable
mothers in Christ, and for the venerable and most blessed mother and

---

100. Zanacchi adopts an old Christian saying, dating perhaps to the fourth century, that a
monk's duty is to mourn, not to teach.

my advocate, the aforesaid holy Ursulina, over whose tomb I, absent in body but present in spirit, resolved to scatter these flowers of her virtuous life in place of an epitaph.[101] It did not seem to me that the time was spent without profit, seeing that I have labored (according to the limits of my small talent) to entrust to written memory, for the use and benefit of posterity, praise, and the virtuous example of so great and venerable a virgin. If I have not kept due measure, then love is responsible, for when love is true, it knows no limit in the service of good works. I trust—let anyone who wants to rebuke me do so—that nonetheless this my filial service and pious zeal for you will be welcome because of your kindness and affection toward me. It will be more than enough for me, even if I am criticized by others, to know that I have done something pleasing to you.

49. Therefore, my sweetest mothers in Christ, accept from the hand of my heart, your poor little servant, this my tiny little gift, a present penned by me in rustic style at love's command—not only in memory and honor of our most beloved mother the blessed virgin Ursulina, but also for your sake. Love me as your son and humble servant because I truly love you in Christ with my whole heart. I beg you, draw yourselves forth to me in deepest love, because my heart is wholly stretched forth to you. Remember me always in your holy prayers, in which I place great hope and trust. As a humble supplicant, I pray the omnipotent and most devout God that he pour forth such blessing and plenitude of holiness over you for your time on this earthly pilgrimage so that following the footsteps of the aforesaid venerable and most saintly virgin Ursulina and one after another ending the course of this mortal life, you have earned sanctification in churches, just as she is doubtless sanctified to whom this phrase of the Apostle can be most justly adapted: God knew her from the beginning and predestined her to be molded in the image of His son [Rom 8:29]. For whom he predestined he also called, and whom he called he also made righteous, and whom he made righteous he also glorified, that is, he made her glorious in holiness. May the God of hope fill you, most devoted mothers in Christ, with every joy and peace until you abound in hope and the strength of the Holy Spirit. Amen.

---

101. The author means that he can offer this account of Ursulina's life and virtues from his monastery, distant from Parma.

50. The holy and venerable body of the nurturing virgin Ursulina was buried in the church of San Giovanni in Verona.[102] A year and a half later, her mother had the body honorably transferred to Parma. It was whole and untouched, marred by absolutely no decay or corruption; instead, it was fragrant with a wonderful sweetness. Bertolina placed it in the church of your monastery of San Quintino, to great popular acclaim, so that you might always see it. When, after four days and four nights, the crowd allowed the blessed body to be buried in the church, the Lord granted the whole populace be shown, through numerous miracles, how He had embraced the most blessed virgin. I will recount a few of the many miracles to offer certain testimony of how pleasing to God was the blessed virgin.

51. The abbess of your monastery of San Quintino, unconvinced of the holiness of the blessed one, made sport of her to all.[103] By God's leave she was entirely deprived of her hearing on the day before the body of the blessed virgin was brought to her church. Once the body had entered the church, the nuns intimated to the abbess by gestures and signs, as best they could, that she should approach the holy body with reverence. For they knew without a doubt that this had happened by divine judgment because she had cursed the blessed virgin and her life. The abbess, persevering in her hardheadedness, rashly mocked the nuns communicating the message, but in order to satisfy their insistence and overcome by their entreaties, she went into the church where the venerable body of the blessed Ursulina lay. She did not approach it, but sat down a ways off in the choir. One of the nuns, who had by chance been detained longer than the others in worship of the relics, standing behind the abbess touched every part of the face of the blessed Ursulina with a reed, in great devotion. Without the abbess knowing, the nun then touched her on the ears from behind with the same reed; the abbess at once recovered her former powers of hearing. The abbess, moved by the novelty of such a miracle, instantly prostrated herself before the relics of the blessed Ursulina, humbly beseeching pardon for her prolonged disbelief and

102. The building that was Ursulina's first mausoleum dates to the twelfth century, although there had been a church on the site in Verona since the early Middle Ages. The handsome Romanesque edifice still stands.

103. This first miracle Zanacchi recounts shows that Ursulina was a controversial figure in her own lifetime, and not merely among her implacable enemies in Avignon. Skepticism always accompanies claims of divine revelation, and Ursulina's tiny stature may have made her an even more likely object of derision.

offering up great thanksgiving to God and the blessed virgin for the blessing granted her.

52. A certain German, thrown into jail for his offenses, was set to be executed the next day when a certain woman who took very ill the prospect of this man's death prostrated herself before the venerable relics of the blessed Ursulina. Pouring forth a flood of tears, she said, "I beg you, most pious virgin, and I earnestly plead, that if you were chosen by God, as everyone says, and if you have found grace in the sight of God, that you seek God's mercy lest this poor and dreadfully unfortunate man, condemned to a capital sentence, perish. Let him, by your merits, obtain God's grace." Wondrous outcome and truly to be greatly marveled at! The man who was to suffer death the next day was freed and allowed to go, unharmed.

While the blessed Ursulina was still living, a certain woman had asked Bertolina to get her daughter to pray on her behalf, to intercede to the Lord for her so that she deserve to conceive children, for she was sterile. When the blessed Ursulina had asked for this favor, a few days later the woman conceived as she had hoped.

53. A certain maiden who had been a servant and intimate of the blessed Ursulina when she was living was forcibly engaged to a man by her parents, even though she had consecrated her immaculate and holy body to the Lord by vow and hoped with the greatest zeal to keep her chastity.[104] This virgin, deprived of all aid, applied to the blessed Ursulina as a last and unique resort as the marriage day approached. In the privacy of her own bedroom, the woman implored the blessed virgin in words of this sort: "If I may be certain, virgin most chaste and pleasing to God, that your intercessions before God are both many and successful, then I beg you, I beseech you, and with my whole heart I miserably and unhappily pray you, and I also entreat you through the merciful heart of our Lord Jesus Christ, that you whom I so completely loved while alive deem it worthy to intercede for me with that same

---

104. In the Middle Ages, the question of marriage alliance was generally one of family interests rather than individual choice. This may explain in part the attraction of the monastic life to women, although often family strategies sent some women as unwillingly into religion as others went into marriage. Following the usual pattern in late medieval Italy, it is likely that the woman (whose youth is stressed later in the story of the miracle) was a teenager engaged to a man she did not know who was considerably older than she was. See Herlihy, *Medieval Households*, 103–11, 144. She is also typical, in her vow of virginity, refusal to marry, and conflict with parents, of a budding saint. See Michael Goodich, "Childhood and Adolescence among the Thirteenth-Century Saints," *History of Childhood Quarterly* 1 (1973), 285–307. Ursulina herself does not fit this pattern.

Jesus Christ, when you are face to face, that if it is right and possible (for with God all things are possible [Mt 19:26]) I not be joined to this mortal spouse, to whom I have been promised, although unwilling. Let me keep myself pure and chaste for your eternal spouse, our Lord Jesus Christ, to whom I long since devoted myself with all my soul and body. Once again now with you as witness—if you do not scorn to stand by me, a wretched sinner—I pledge to keep myself pure and chaste as long as I live, by the favor of that same Lord Jesus Christ and with the support of your merits. Come now, blessed virgin, accept the appeals of this your wretched and devoted albeit sinful servant; hear my prayers; see the tears and bitter sobs I now pour out. I beg, and again I beg, do not allow the tears that I have brought forth from a very bitter heart to be returned to me unfulfilled. For while living you taught us to be compassionate to the wretched and have mercy on the afflicted; how much more, sitting there in glory, should you be compassionate and have mercy, for all my hope is in you, and I hope to fulfill my every vow through you. Alas for miserable, miserable me! Oh, blessed virgin, make haste to console me! I await your aid, I hope for your help, and I am sure, most pious one, that you will not disdain so many prayers and tears, such bitter sobbing and sighing. Come, hurry to rescue me from such terrible misery and irrevocable misfortune."

54. As soon as she had finished the prayer along these lines, the blessed Ursulina appeared to her, dressed just as the young woman had been accustomed to see her in life, only much more beautiful. Terrified, she did not dare to gaze directly at the virgin's visage. When Ursulina saw how she was shaking, she said, "Do not be afraid, sister, for look, I am here, the one whom you so beseeched. Be of good cheer, my beloved sister and co-heir to the eternal kingdom: for now, rejoice and exult in our bridegroom, the Lord Jesus Christ. Be joyful, sister, for your plea and copious tears have passed through the clouds, crossed the skies and the golden stars, and finally reached the sight of the divine majesty. Be joyful now, because our Lord Jesus Christ, the true and eternal bridegroom, accedes to your wish and calls you to eternal marriage. On the coming Sunday you will rejoice with us in perpetual glory." This pronouncement was made on Wednesday before the Sunday on which the young woman went off to her eternal marriage—and that her parents had set as the date for the consummation of earthly nuptials. Once she had spoken these things, the blessed Ursulina disappeared from human sight. The young woman was filled with every joy and sweetness, reminding herself

silently every hour and moment that the date of her death had been set and never ceasing to give the worthiest thanks she could to God and the blessed virgin. The one she had petitioned fulfilled her vow even more fully than she had promised. On that very day, the young woman began to suffer fever. Fitful heat ran through all her weakened limbs and shook to the foundation all the senses and strengths of her little body. But she bore everything with calmness, since she was shortly to delight in the eternal kingdom, suffering gladly but even more gladly awaiting rewards to come. At once she quelled terrible illness with the hope of glory to come and paid for perpetual reward with short-lived pain. Until that Sunday a few days after the vision of the blessed Ursulina, the young woman was burdened with fever, filled with pain, and greatly afflicted in her body, but she remained of cheerful mind. At the hour foretold to her by the blessed Ursulina, she delivered her soul to the Lord Jesus Christ, with whom she will reign forever and ever. Amen.

55. A certain young man was in the grip of a grave illness and nearly at the point of death when his mother, who bore her child's illness unhappily, invoked the holy virgin Ursulina. Having quickly recovered his strength, he was fully freed from illness in a short time.

A woman of Verona was washing a linen cloth in a river when it slipped out of her hands; trying to recover it, she was drawn along with the cloth by the force of the current. Seeing herself in danger of drowning, she invoked Ursulina, and at once through her agency the woman and her wash were brought back to dry land, freed from the aforementioned peril.

A certain woman named Catherine suffered so in her eyes that she was nearly blind in one and did not leave her house for shame. She called on the virgin, who appeared to her that very night and said, "Go to Mass in the morning and you will be freed." And so it happened, just as the virgin Ursulina had foretold.

56. A nun in Venice was utterly in thrall to the devil, to the point that she put aside her religious habit and attached herself to a young man. She was reduced to the point of wanting to flee the monastery altogether in the company of this youth.[105] The nun's mother, a devotee of the sacred virgin Ursulina, knew about this and despaired of her daughter's honor. She hastened to the blessed virgin Ursulina and pleaded with her to obtain from the Lord constancy for

---

105. The woman had perhaps not taken her final and lifelong vows, signaling her intention not to do so by refusing to wear religious garb.

her daughter and banish this very wicked temptation from her heart. The blessed Ursulina entered her chapel and prayed for the nun; when she departed, she gave the nun's mother a scrap of writing for her daughter to read. It read: What delights is momentary, but what tortures is eternal. When the nun had read it, she was at once made steadfast. Carrying out her original intention, she served the Lord to the end of her life and died in peace. Amen.[106]

57. Reverend Mother and dearest mothers in Christ, I have decided it more worthy to leave to you to hear and add the numerous other miracles God worked through the merits of this most holy virgin Ursulina than to narrate them inadequately and in unpolished style. Therefore, most devoted mothers in Christ, from these few words we should ponder that there is much more: both Ursulina's wondrous life and famous habits and her holy way of life. Taught by such an example, may we obtain that eternal blessedness in which the blessed virgin herself rejoices with God the Father, His Son our Lord Jesus Christ, and the Holy Spirit, to whom be praise, honor, power, and dominion through the ages. Amen.

Here ends the brief description of the life of the most blessed virgin Ursulina of Parma, most magnificent spouse of Jesus Christ. Done on the feast of the Ten Thousand Virgins, October 1472.[107]

106. This story seems to date from Ursulina's stay in Venice (section 33) during her lifetime. Pope Boniface had permitted Ursulina to have a private chapel in her dwelling (see section 29). The proverb Ursulina sends is a medieval commonplace, attributed variously to St. Augustine and St. Gregory the Great (whom the author quotes elsewhere in the *vita*) but unknown in any of their surviving works.

107. Zanacchi chooses a particularly apt date. The ten (sometimes eleven) thousand virgins of old Christian legend, martyrs to pagan Huns, were led by St. Ursula, of which "Ursulina" is a diminutive. Ursula refused to allow her Christian companions to be enslaved by the pagan leaders or give up their faith, so they were all killed and immediately accepted into heaven. Like Ursula, Ursulina confronted powerful male authorities with great confidence.

I. Pope Boniface IX allows Ursulina to choose a confessor who will be able to grant her deathbed pardon for all her sins

Bishop Boniface, servant of the servants of God, to his beloved daughter in Christ Ursulina, daughter of Pietro Veneri, a woman of Parma: greetings and apostolic blessing.

It proceeds from the loving devotion with which you regard us and the Roman Church, that we allow the grace of a favorable reply to your requests, especially those concerning the salvation of your soul. Thus it is that we, attending to your pleas, bestow on your devotion this favor in the present words: that a confessor of your choice be allowed to grant you once only, at the moment of death, full remission for all the sins you have confessed with contrite heart and voice, in sincerity of faith, the unity of the Holy Roman Church, and obedience and devotion to us and to our successors lawfully entering the Roman pontificate with enduring apostolic authority. Nevertheless, the same confessor should demand satisfaction from you concerning those matters in which satisfaction is to be made to someone else, if you survive, or from your heirs if by then you have passed on, which amends you or they shall be required to make, as stated.[1] And lest, God forbid, on account of this favor you become more inclined to sinful acts hereafter, we desire that if by chance you commit sin in the confidence of this remission, then by no means should pardon be granted to you for what you have done.[2]

Therefore let nobody whosoever interfere with this page expressing our permission and will, or oppose it with impertinent daring. If anyone presumes to attempt it, let him know he will incur the wrath of almighty God and the blessed apostles Peter and Paul. Given in Rome, at St. Peter's, on the ninth kalends of March in the seventh year of our pontificate.[3]

1. The apparent meaning is that if any promise of material offering is associated with this process of confession and remission of sins, Ursulina or her heirs are obliged to fulfill it.

2. The pope, then, puts two important limits on the grant that Ursulina's chosen confessor be able to pardon all her sins after deathbed confession: she is not to use this privilege as a license to ignore earthly obligations nor abuse it by sinning consciously in the expectation of full pardon.

3. February 21, 1396.

II. Pope Boniface IX allows Ursulina and her mother to lead a party of ten other pilgrims to the Holy Land

Bishop Boniface, servant of the servants of God, to his beloved daughters in Christ Bertolina, widow of the layman Pietro Veneri, and their daughter Ursulina, a native of Parma: greeting and apostolic blessing.

We freely grant your desires, as your meritorious devotion demands, in that we reply favorably to your pleas—especially with relation to things you honorably seek—insofar as we, with God, are able to do. Therefore, since the petition you offered to us includes the statement that you both, burning with the zeal of pious devotion, urgently desire to travel abroad and visit in person the Holy Sepulcher and other churches in the Holy Land, we, attending to your supplications in this matter, permit you for this reason to visit the Tomb and the other aforementioned churches with ten other people to be chosen whom one or both of you will guide. Certain prohibitions, decrees, and processes of the Apostolic See to the contrary made or even published, containing punishments and spiritual or temporal sentences, shall by no means impede you.[4] For the sake of such a visit you should be able to bring along and even display things without which you would be unable to undertake such a journey. As long as you and similar people neither bring nor cause to be brought anything else to those places that might redound to the profit or favor of the enemies of the Christian faith,[5] we grant permission to you and those persons by the authority of these words.

4. Women had become pilgrims to Jerusalem as early as the fourth century and almost as early had become the target of criticism. They were often thought frivolous, a threat to male pilgrims' virtue, or a nuisance requiring special accommodations. See Anna Benvenuti, "Donne sulla strada: l'itineranza religiosa femminile nel Medioevo," in *Donne in viaggio. Viaggio religioso, politico, metaforico*, ed. Maria Luisa Silvestre and Adriana Valerio (Rome: Laterza, 1999), 74–86. Concerning criticism of female pilgrims see Sumption, *Pilgrimage*, 261–63 and Ursula Ganz-Blättler, *Andacht und Abenteuer. Berichte europäischer Jerusalem—und Santiago-Pilger (1320–1520)* (Tübingen: G. Narr, 1990), 325–26. See also Leigh Ann Craig, "'Stronger than Men and Braver than Knights': Women and the Pilgrimages to Jerusalem and Rome in the Later Middle Ages," *Journal of Medieval History* 29 (2003), 153–75, esp. the section "Femininity as liability in pilgrimage groups," 162–70.

5. The pope's meaning is not quite clear here. Probably the things to which he refers are money, supplies, and even devotional items that pilgrims might want to take or have visible as they visited the holy places. Given risks pilgrims to the Holy Land were said to face—robbery, enslavement, and worse at the hand of the local Muslim population ("the enemies of the Christian faith")—it would not be surprising for Boniface to urge due caution about suitably modest provisioning that would keep the party from becoming a target.

Therefore, let no one whosoever interfere with this document expressing our permission or oppose it with impertinent daring. If anyone presumes to attempt it, let him know he will incur the wrath of almighty God and the blessed apostles Peter and Paul. Given in Rome, at St. Peter's, on the kalends of March in the seventh year of our pontificate.[6]

6. March 1, 1396.

I. Primary Sources

Augustine. Sermo LXIX. PL 38: 440–42.

Bonet, Honoré. *L'Arbre des batailles*. Edited by Ernest Nys. Brussels: Librairie Européenne, 1883.

Bovet. See Bonet

Bridget [Birgitta] of Sweden. *Revelationes: Book IV*. Edited by Hans Aili. Stockholm: Almqvist and Wiksell, 1992.

The Chartae of the Carthusian General Chapter: Paris, Bibliothèque Nationale MS Latin 10888, Part I, (ff. 1–157v). Edited by Michael Sargent and James Hogg. Salzburg: Institut für Anglistik und Amerikanistik, Universität Salzburg, 1985.

La cronaca della Certosa del Montello. Edited by Maria Luisa Crovato. Padua: Antenore, 1987.

Fasti Ecclesiae Anglicanae, 1300–1541: Monastic Cathedrals (Southern Province). Compiled by B. Jones. Vol. 4 of *Fasti Ecclesiae Anglicanae, 1300–1541*, edited by John Le Neve. London: Institute of Historical Research, 1962–67.

Gregory the Great. *Dialogues*. Edited by Adalbert de Vogüé and translated by Paul Antin. 3 vols. Paris: Cerf, 1978–80.

Gregory the Great. Homilia VII. PL 76: 1099–1103.

The Letters of Catherine of Siena. Edited by Suzanne Noffke. 2 vols. Tempe: Arizona Center for Medieval and Renaissance Studies, 2000.

Raymond de Sabanac, ["The *Revelations* of Constance of Rabastens"]. In Noël Valois and Amédée Pagès, "Les Révélations de Constance de Rabastens et le Schisme d'Occident (1384–86)." *Annales du Midi* 8 (1896): 249–78.

La Vengeance de Nostre-Seigneur. Edited by Alvin E. Ford. Toronto: Pontifical Institute of Mediaeval Studies, 1984.

Zanacchi, Simone. "Vita [Beatae Ursulinae]." In AASS, April vol. 1, cols. 725–39.

II. Secondary Sources

Affò, Ireneo. *Vita della Beata Orsolina da Parma*. Parma: Reale, 1786.

Andersson, Aron. *St. Birgitta and the Holy Land*. Stockholm: The Museum of National Antiquities, 1973.

Astarita, Tommaso. *Between Salt Water and Holy Water: A History of Southern Italy*. New York: Norton, 2005.

Behringer, Wolfgang. "How Waldensians became Witches: Heretics and their Journey to the Other World." In *Communicating with the Spirits*, edited by Gábor Klaniczay and Eva Pócs, 155–92. Budapest and New York: CEU Press, 2005.

Benvenuti, Anna. "Donne sulla strada: l'itineranza religiosa femminile nel Medioevo." In *Donne in viaggio. Viaggio religioso, politico, metaforico*, edited by Maria Luisa Silvestre and Adriana Valerio, 74–86. Rome: Laterza, 1999.

Bernini, Ferdinando. *Storia di Parma*. 2nd ed. Parma: L. Battei, 1976.

Bibliotheca sanctorum, 13 vols. Rome: Pontificia Università lateranense, 1961–1970.

Bilinkoff, Jodi. *Related Lives: Confessors and Their Female Penitents, 1450–1750*. Ithaca: Cornell University Press, 2005.

Blumenfeld-Kosinski, Renate. "Constance de Rabastens and the Discernment of Spirits." In *Medieval Christianity in Practice*, edited by Miri Rubin. Princeton: Princeton University Press, 2009, 290–95.

_____. *Poets, Saints, and Visionaries of the Great Schism, 1378–1417*. University Park: Pennsylvania State University Press, 2006.

_____. "Visions and Schism Politics in the Twelfth Century: Hildegard of Bingen, John of Salisbury, and Elisabeth of Schönau." In *Saints, Scholars, and Politicians: Gender as a Tool in Medieval Studies*, edited by Mathilde van Dijk and Renée Nip, 173–87. Turnhout: Brepols, 2005.

Bornstein, Daniel. "Women and Religion in Late Medieval Italy: History and Historiography." In *Women and Religion in Medieval and Renaissance Italy*, edited by Daniel Bornstein and Roberto Rusconi, 1–27. Chicago: University of Chicago Press, 1996.

Brody, Saul. *The Disease of the Soul: Leprosy in Medieval Literature*. Ithaca: Cornell University Press, 1974.

Burr, David. "Antichrist and Islam in Medieval Franciscan Exegesis." In *Medieval Christian Perceptions of Islam: A Book of Essays*, edited by John V. Tolan, 131–52. New York: Garland, 1996.

Bynum, Caroline Walker. *Holy Feast and Holy Fast: The Religious Significance of Food to Medieval Women*. Berkeley: University of California Press, 1987.

Caciola, Nancy. *Discerning Spirits: Divine and Demonic Possession in the Middle Ages*. Ithaca: Cornell University Press, 2003.

Chareyron, Nicole. *Pilgrims to Jerusalem in the Middle Ages*. Translated by W. Donald Wilson. New York: Columbia University Press, 2005.

Coakley, John W. *Women, Men, and Spiritual Power: Female Saints and Their Male Collaborators*. New York: Columbia University Press, 2006.

Craig, Leigh Ann. "'Stronger than Men and Braver than Knights': Women and the Pilgrimages to Jerusalem and Rome in the Later Middle Ages." *Journal of Medieval History* 29 (2003), 153–75.

Dall'Aglio, Italo. *La Diocesi di Parma*. 2 vols. Parma: Scuola Tipografica Benedettina, 1966.

Dall'Acqua, Marzio. "Il Monastero di San Paolo." In *Il Monastero di San Paolo*, edited by Marzio Dall'Acqua, 11–42. Parma: Franco Maria Ricci, 1990.

Delehaye, Hippolyte. *The Legends of the Saints: An Introduction to Hagiography*. Translated by V. M. Crawford. Notre Dame: University of Notre Dame Press, 1961.

Dinzelbacher, Peter. *Mittelalterliche Frauenmystik*. Paderborn: F. Schöningh, 1993.

Dronke, Peter. "Tradition and Innovation in Mediaeval Western Colour Imagery." *Eranos Jahrbuch* 41 (1972), 51–107.

Elliott, Dyan. *Proving Woman: Female Spirituality and Inquisitional Culture in the Later Middle Ages*. Princeton: Princeton University Press, 2004.

Emmerson, Richard K. *Antichrist in the Middle Ages: A Study of Medieval Apocalypticism, Art, and Literature*. Seattle: University of Washington Press, 1981.

Frazier, Alison Knowles. *Possible Lives: Authors and Saints in Renaissance Italy*. New York: Columbia University Press, 2005.

Gallo, Donato. "Dalla Certosa del Montello alla Certosa de Vedana: La Fortuna dei certosini nell'ambiente veneto del Tre-Quattrocento." In *La Certosa di Vedana*, edited by L. S. Magoga and F. Marin, 7–21. Florence: Olschki, 1998.

Ganz-Blättler, Ursula. *Andacht und Abenteuer. Berichte europäischer Jerusalem- und Santiago-Pilger (1320–1520)*. Tübingen: G. Narr, 1990.

Gentile, Marco. *Terra e Poteri: Parma e il Parmense nel ducato visconteo all'inizio del Quattrocento*. Milan: Unicopli, 2001.

Goodich, Michael. "Childhood and Adolescence among the Thirteenth-Century Saints." *History of Childhood Quarterly* 1 (1973), 285–307.

Gruys, Albert. *Cartusiana*. 3 vols. Paris: CNRS, 1976–78.

Guenée, Bernard. *L'opinion publique à la fin du Moyen Age d'après la "Chronique de Charles VI" du Religieux de Saint-Denis*. Paris: Perrin, 2002.

Harthan, John. *The Book of Hours*. New York: Thomas Y. Crowell, 1977.

Hasenohr, Geneviève. "*Lacrymae pondera vocis habent*. Typologie des larmes dans la littérature de spiritualité française des XIII–XVe siècles." *Le Moyen Français* 37 (1997), 45–63.

Heffernan, Thomas J. *Sacred Biography: Saints and Their Biographers in the Middle Ages*. New York: Oxford University Press, 1988.

Herlihy, David. *Medieval Households*. Cambridge: Harvard University Press, 1985.

Hierarchia Catholica Medii Aevi. 2nd ed. 8 volumes. Monasterii: Libraria Regensbergiana, 1913–78.

Hiver-Bérenguier, Jean-Pierre. *Constance de Rabastens: Mystique de Dieu ou de Gaston Febus?* Toulouse: Privat, 1984.

Housley, Norman. *The Later Crusades, 1274–1580: From Lyons to Alacazar*. Oxford: Oxford University Press, 1992.

Luongo, F. Thomas. *The Saintly Politics of Catherine of Siena*. Ithaca: Cornell University Press, 2005.

Maisonneuve, Roland. "L'expérience mystique et visionnaire de Marguerite d'Oingt." In *Kartäusermystik und -Mystiker*, edited by James Hogg, 81–102. Salzburg: Institut für Anglistik und Amerikanistik, Universität Salzburg, 1981.

McIver, Katherine. "Nuns' Habits: Negotiating Power Behind Convent Walls." Paper presented at the annual meeting of the Renaissance Society of America, Cambridge, England, April 2005.

Mooney, Catherine M., ed. *Gendered Voices: Medieval Saints and Their Interpreters.* Philadelphia: University of Pennsylvania Press, 1999.

Moreira, Isabel. *Dreams, Visions, and Spiritual Authority in Merovingian Gaul.* Ithaca: Cornell University Press, 2000.

Nagy, Piroska. *Le don des larmes au Moyen Age: Un instrument spirituel en quête d'institution (Ve–XIIIe siècle).* Paris: Albin Michel, 2000.

Newman, Barbara. "What Did it Mean to Say 'I Saw'? The Clash between Theory and Practice in Medieval Visionary Culture." *Speculum* 80 (2005), 1–43.

Ohler, Norbert. *The Medieval Traveller.* Translated by Caroline Hillier. Woodbridge: Boydell, 1995.

Pesce, Luigi. "Filippo di Mézières e la Certosa del Montello." *Archivio veneto* ser. 5, no. 168, vol. 134 (1990), 5–44.

Poor, Sara S. *Mechthild of Magdeburg and Her Book: Gender and the Making of Textual Authority.* Philadelphia: University of Pennsylvania Press, 2004.

Rigon, Antonio. "Amici padovani del Petrarca e il monastero di S. Maria della Riviera." *Studi petrarcheschi* n.s. 6 (1989), 241–55.

Rowland, Beryl. *Birds with Human Souls: A Guide to Bird Symbolism.* Knoxville: University of Tennessee Press, 1978.

Sahlin, Claire L. *Birgitta of Sweden and the Voice of Prophecy.* Rochester, NY: Boydell Press, 2001.

Smoller, Laura A. "Holy Mothers: The History of a Designation of Spiritual Status." In *Piety and Family in Early Modern Europe*, edited by Marc R. Forster and Benjamin J. Kaplan, 178–200. Burlington: Ashgate, 2005.

Sumption, Jonathan. *Pilgrimage: An Image of Mediaeval Religion.* Totowa, NJ: Rowman and Littlefield, 1975.

Thorndike, Lynn. *A History of Magic and Experimental Science.* 8 vols. New York: Columbia University Press, 1923–58.

Tobin, Matthew. "Les Visions et révélations de Marie Robine d'Avignon dans le contexte prophétique des années 1400." In *Fin du monde et signes des temps. Visionnaires et prophètes en France méridionale (fin XIIIe-début XVe siècle). Cahiers de Fanjeaux* 27 (1992), 309–29."

Tolan, John V. *Saracens: Islam in the Medieval European Imagination.* New York: Columbia University Press, 2002.

Tucoo-Chala, Pierre. *Gaston Fébus et la vicomté de Béarn, 1343–1391.* Bordeaux: Bière, 1959.

Ullmann, Walter. *The Origins of the Great Schism.* London: Burns, Oates & Washbourne, 1948.

Utterback, Kristine T. "The Vision Becomes Reality: Medieval Women Pilgrims to the Holy Land." In *Pilgrims and Travelers to the Holy Land*, edited by Bryan F. Le Beau and Menachem Mor, 159–68. Omaha: Creighton University Press, 1996.

Valois, Noël. *La France et le Grand Schisme d'Occident.* 4 vols. Paris: A. Picard, 1896–1902.

Valois, Noël and Amédée Pagès. "Les Révélations de Constance de Rabastens et le Schisme d'Occident (1384–86)." *Annales du Midi* 8 (1896), 241–78.

Vauchez, André. *The Laity in the Middle Ages: Religious Beliefs and Devotional Practice.* Translated by Margery J. Schneider. Notre Dame: University of Notre Dame Press, 1993.

Webb, Diana. *Medieval European Pilgrimage, c. 700–c. 1500.* New York: Palgrave, 2002.

Zarri, Gabriella. "Living Saints: A Typology of Female Sanctity in the Early Sixteenth Century." In *Women and Religion in Medieval and Renaissance Italy*, edited by Daniel Bornstein and Roberto Rusconi, 219–303. Chicago: University of Chicago Press, 1996.

Marquis Book Printing Inc.

Québec, Canada

2010